The War on People who Use Drugs

This book explores the outcomes of Sweden's aim to create a 'drug-free society' on the lived realities, health, and welfare of people who use drugs, and on the dynamics of Swedish drug use. Drawing on a wealth of empirical data, including extensive interview testimony and participant observation from years of fieldwork conducted in Sweden, the book debunks the widely believed myth that Sweden is a progressive, liberal, inclusive state. In contrast to its liberal reputation, Sweden has criminalised the use of drugs and allows for compulsory treatment for those with drug dependencies. The work argues that Swedish law and policy cannot be demonstrated to have decreased drug use as intended, with the law used instead as a means by which to displace people who use drugs from public spaces in Sweden's cities. And where the law has failed in its ambition to decrease drug use, Swedish law and policy have increased and exacerbated the problems, dangers, and harms that can be associated with it. People who use drugs in Sweden experience considerable and endemic difficulties with health, violence, abuse, and social exclusion, stigma, and discrimination as a result of Sweden's drug laws, policies, and discourses.

Jay Levy's work, writing, advocacy, fieldwork, and research interests include the outcomes of drug and sex work legislation and discourse; feminist, gender, and queer theory; harm reduction, HIV/AIDS, STI, and blood-borne infection policy and law. He has worked with the African Medical and Research Foundation (AMREF), as a consultant for the Global Network of Sex Work Projects (NSWP), with the International Network of People who Use Drugs (INPUD) Secretariat, and as a supervisor for undergraduates at the University of Cambridge, where he completed his PhD at the Department of Geography. His first monograph, *Criminalising the Purchase of Sex: Lessons from Sweden*, was also published by Routledge.

'Jay Levy's compelling study should be mandatory reading for anyone who still harbours the notion that Sweden is a progressive paragon. Compulsory blood testing, police harassment, child custody used as leverage, basic services made arbitrary and conditional: Levy counts the costs, and the casualties, of Sweden's search for a "drug-free society".'

Dr Philip Howell, Senior Lecturer, Department of Geography,
University of Cambridge

'Levy's insightful and well-written analysis of the harms of Swedish drug policy exposes the underlying common rationales between the history of social engineering and the nation's war on drugs. Rigorously researched and excellently written, the book ultimately advances understandings of drug use and people who use them, effectively outlining the reasons why we must re-imagine our approaches to drugs, drug use, and the people that use drugs in new and radical ways.'

Judy Chang, Executive Director, International Network of
People who Use Drugs (INPUD)

The War on People who Use Drugs

The Harms of Sweden's Aim for a Drug-free Society

Jay Levy

Routledge
Taylor & Francis Group
LONDON AND NEW YORK

First published 2018
by Routledge

2 Park Square, Milton Park, Abingdon, Oxfordshire OX14 4RN
52 Vanderbilt Avenue, New York, NY 10017

Routledge is an imprint of the Taylor & Francis Group, an informa business

First issued in paperback 2020

British Library Cataloguing-in-Publication Data
A catalogue record for this book is available from the British Library

Library of Congress Cataloging-in-Publication Data
A catalog record for this book has been requested

ISBN: 978-1-4724-8785-8 (hbk)
ISBN: 978-0-367-59485-5 (pbk)

Typeset in Galliard
by Taylor & Francis Books

Contents

Figures

Acknowledgements

I am enormously grateful to many people for their support of me and my work, both in Sweden, and abroad, people without whom this book – let alone much of the rest of my work – would not have been possible. I should begin at the beginning, by thanking all of those wonderful people who gave me but a glimpse of what it is to live in Sweden, for enriching my Swedish life, and for all of the memories and lasting friendships. Particularly, I want to thank Patrick, Frida, Johan, Sandra, Carina, Victoria, Tobias, Jimmy, Matilda, Anton, Alex, Stefan, Tina, Ulrika, Naomi, Ricard, Rima, Danny, Daniel, Pernilla, and – most importantly – Pye. What a window into Swedish life to look through!

For advice and feedback directly related to this book, the research that informed it, and my PhD and other writings and papers that precede it, I chiefly want to thank my father, Richard Levy, whose constructive criticism, generosity of time, feedback, and patience have been utterly indispensable to me through the years. My mother's feedback and service as a sounding board has also been hugely helpful! In addition, I must thank Matthew Weait for such helpful feedback and time for many years; Matthew's generosity has been both moving and vital, both to me, and in so many areas of academic work and activism. I would also like to thank – for direct and indirect help with my writing, work, and general reflections – Roisin Ellison, Celia St.John-Green, Adam Levy, Toni Stone, Luca Stevenson, Yiğit Aydinalp, Thierry Schaffauser, Petra Östergren, Chris Lewis, Caighli Taylor, Sam Greenbury, Luke Pagarani, Emily Heavey, Andy Wright, Eliot Albers, Sofie Buckland, Valentin Simionov, Terry White, Humy Zaman, Geoff Gedroyc, Reema Mehta, Shaun Shelly, Hannah Lewis, Judy Chang, Stephen Malloy, Brun González, and Geoff Ward. Especial and enormous thanks (again) to Pye Jakobsson also, whose time and friendship were the fundamental foundation of the time I spent in Sweden. As with my previous book, my work, such as it was in Sweden, would not have been possible were it not for her. I would like to give huge thanks additionally to Berne Stålenkrantz and the Swedish and Stockholm Drug Users Unions (*Svenska Brukarföreningen*), and also to RFHL and RNS for the level of access granted to me by their organisations, and also specifically Morten Sortodden and Linda Byqvist for their hospitality and guidance during fieldwork in Oslo and Malmö respectively.

Those who have given me academic guidance, direction, supervision, and generosity of their acumen deserve special thanks, particularly my supervisor at

Cambridge, Phil Howell, for his insightful academic supervision during the course of my Master's and PhD research, not to mention my formative years as an undergraduate student. Steve Trudgill – my old Director of Studies – deserves special thanks too, as does Jim Duncan, both of whom enriched my academic learning as an undergraduate student, developing my understanding, passion, and interest for such a dynamic, varied, and fascinating subject. Thanks also to Gerry Kearns, both for his guidance and supervision as an undergraduate student, and also for his thoughtful and incisive supervision during my MPhil. Thanks also go to Phil Hubbard and Belinda Brooks-Gordon for your perspective on my work during and following my PhD viva. A word of thanks too to David Watson, in the Cartography Unit of the Cambridge University Geography Department, for his cartographic contributions to my PhD and to this book.

I also, of course, thank the Economic and Social Research Council; without their generous funding, my MPhil and PhD research would have been impossible and so, too, would this book. I am hugely appreciative of their support. Where this book stems from elements of my PhD, elements of my PhD's literature review were reworked into a short booklet in 2013, *The Harms of Drug Use: Criminalisation, Misinformation, and Stigma* (Levy 2013); this, circularly, was reworked back into small facets of this book.

I would like to thank all of my respondents for their great generosity and for taking the time to candidly and munificently contribute to my research; in particular, I would like to give specific and heartfelt thanks to the people who use drugs who took the time to talk with me and share their stories, views, ideas, research, testimony, and tireless activism. So my first dedication is to all of the people who use drugs and the psychonauts who contributed to this book, my research, and continue to enrich my life. Thank you for everything.

And my second dedication is to my brother, Adam Levy, and my partner, Celia St.John-Green. I know to whom to turn when things get rough. Thank you both.

Glossary, acronyms, and abbreviations

AIDS	Acquired Immunodeficiency Syndrome
Brukarföreningen	'The (Drug) Users Union' (also see *Svenskabrukarföreningen*)
EMCDDA	The European Monitoring Centre for Drugs and Drug Addiction
EU	The European Union
FMN (föräldraföreningen mot narkotika)	'Parents' Association Against Drugs'
Folkhemmet/folkhem	'The People's Home'/'People's Home'
HIV	Human Immunodeficiency Virus
IDU(s)	Injecting Drug User(s)
INPUD	International Network of People who Use Drugs
IOGT-NTO (Independent Order of Good Templars – *nationalgodtemplarorden templarorden*)	NGO working for a sober life
KRIS (*kriminellas revansch i samhallet*)	'Criminals Return into Society'
LVM (*lagen om vård av missbrukare*)	'The Law for the Care of Misusers/Abusers'
OST	Opiate Substitution Therapy (usually methadone or buprenorphine [Subutex])
Plattan	'The Slab'/'The Plate', colloquial name for Sergels Torg Square in central Stockholm, well known as an area where drugs are bought and sold
RFHL (*riksförbundet för hjälp åt narkotika och lä kemedelsberoende*)	'Association for Assistance with Drugs and Drug Dependence'
RNS (*riksförbundet Narkotikafritt Samhälle*)	'Association for a Drug-Free Society'

Sexköpslagen	'The Sex Purchase Law' criminalising the purchase of sex
Socialstyrelsen	'The (Swedish) National Board of Health and Welfare'
STI/STD	Sexually Transmitted Infection/Disease
Subutex	Brand name for buprenorphine, used for opiate substitution therapy
Svenska Brukarföreningen	'The Swedish (Drug) Users Union'
UN	The United Nations
UNAIDS	The Joint United Nations Programme on HIV/AIDS
UNODC	The United Nations Office on Drugs and Crime
WHO	The World Health Organization

Introduction

In 1988 Sweden criminalised the very *use* of drugs,[1] and introduced legislation that allowed for the compulsory detention and 'treatment' of those with drug dependencies. Thus, in Sweden it is a criminal offence to have drugs in one's bloodstream, and being a drug user can result in being medically incarcerated. It is quite literally illegal for people who are currently using drugs to live in Sweden. This diverges from legislation in much of the rest of the European Union, and in many other states besides, that indirectly criminalises people who use drugs through criminalising the activities *surrounding* drug use – possession, intent to supply, and so forth – but not drug use *per se*.

Sweden is a notable voice in the international arena: at a time when some states are beginning to move away from models of criminalisation, Sweden continues to promote criminalisation and policies that exacerbate harm and undermine the agency and self-determination of people who use drugs. And Sweden's international influence is of particular significance; although some states are moving away from criminalising models, this is a time of great fluidity, with other states increasingly moving *away* from 'liberal' models and criminalising the use of drugs, and allowing for compulsory treatment and incarceration for people with drug dependencies, following Sweden's example. Though there has been some research on the genealogy of the legislative debates that resulted in Sweden's prohibitionist drug legislation, as well as research on drug user rights activism in Sweden, little research has focussed on the direct outcomes of Swedish legislation, policy, and discourse[2] on the lives and lived realities of people who use drugs in Sweden. Informed by fieldwork and research conducted in Sweden between 2008 and 2012, this book establishes the origins and outcomes of Sweden's legislation criminalising the use of drugs and providing for the compulsory treatment of people with drug dependencies. The book will principally address the impacts of these laws, focussing on how drugs and the people who use them have come to be socially constructed and understood, establishing and exploring the levels of drug use in Sweden and the dynamics of drug use, and discussing and establishing what the impacts of Sweden's pursuit of punitive prohibition have been upon the lives and experiences of communities of people who use drugs.

Sweden: a bastion of 'liberal' democracy?

To begin with, it is necessary to set the scene. What is Sweden like? How is it to live in Sweden? I have lost count of the number of conversations I have had with people that have begun with something along the lines of '...but I thought Sweden was so liberal, progressive, and forward-thinking!' Sweden is indeed commonly perceived as a bastion of 'liberal'[3] democracy, a society that prioritises individual freedoms, agency, and self-determination of its citizens, autonomy from the state, all whilst protecting the most vulnerable within society through an intricate, sophisticated, extensive, and ostensibly *inclusive* welfare state. Capitalism and socialism in *lagom*[4] amounts. How Swedish!

But I wish to start this book by paraphrasing Don Kulick (2003) in emphasising that these notions of Sweden as an inclusive and liberal utopia are utterly erroneous, misleading, and unhelpful. As I always continue the abovementioned conversations: *Sweden has excellent PR*. Though I have discussed this elsewhere (Levy 2015), an understanding of the stark divergence of Sweden's reality from commonly held misconceptions is imperative to contextualise the following chapters' analyses of repressive Swedish drug legislation and policy: Sweden's welfare state – and how Sweden engages with, and legislates on, marginalised and stigmatised communities – is deeply rooted in Sweden's history of social engineering, eugenics, and projects of modernity and rationalisation. These are projects that have seen groups constructed as deviant, dangerous, and disruptive to normative[5] Swedish society having their freedoms, movements, and bodily integrity heavily curtailed, controlled, and violated. Not so liberal after all!

Eugenics, social engineering, sterilisations, containment, and control

Sweden has aspired to create, to *engineer*, a 'People's Home', or *folkhem* (*folkhemmet* being the definite article, '*the* People's Home'), with this home committed to a high level of welfare, health, full employment of the population, high quality and levels of education, and attendant prosperity and social wellbeing (Anker 2007; Gould 1989; Hallam 2010; Subrahmanian 2007). But these have been top-down projects, with the Swedish state acting as a parent to the people, who have been constructed to be at best irresponsible, at worst recalcitrant, children. As is aptly stressed by Henriksson and Ytterberg (1992: 335), the Swedish 'government, acting as a Good Parent, was driven to look after its children, to assure that they behaved, that they didn't drink too much, that they didn't visit "bad" places, that they were not involved with dangerous sexuality'. An excellent summary of the paternalistic and patronising *folkhemmet.*

During the 19th and 20th centuries, various pieces of legislation have been used in Sweden to control groups believed to destabilise the normative People's Home. Compulsory and medicalised care and treatment have been used as a lens through which to control and contain various communities: mandatory medical examinations for communicable and venereal diseases were directed towards various problematised groups and professions, determined by racist and sexist criteria, through the 1800s. Groups who were subject to these violations of their bodily integrity particularly included women – notably putatively promiscuous women and female sex workers – and the impoverished (Blom 2006; Blom 2007; Svanström 2006). Subsequent venereal disease legislation, which involved inspection, compulsory contact tracing and medical care, and isolation/incarceration (Blom 2006; Lundberg 2006) purported to be gender neutral (Baldwin 1999; Baldwin 2005; Blom 2007; Hubbard et al. 2007a), but again came to focus heavily on women, sex workers, and those considered to be feeble minded, with vagrancy legislation used in tandem with venereal disease legislation to displace, contain, examine, incarcerate, and control these groups (Svanström 2006). The 19th century gave way to the 20th, and Sweden's projects of social engineering came to be informed by newly emergent eugenic discourse, with the resultant social hygiene projects (Svanström 2006) fed substantively by Alva and Gunnar Myrdal's ideas as to how – and for whom – the *folkhemmet* should be engineered (Ekerwald 2001; Gould 2005). These were eugenic projects rivalled on scale by only those of Nazi Germany (Baldwin 2005), with over 60,000 people, constructed as eugenically deficient, feebleminded, and/or disabled, sterilised by the Swedish state, with at least 21,000 of these sterilisations being forced or coerced (SOU 2000: 20). I want to emphasise that these are not historical projects. They have continued into living memory: widespread sterilisations continued until the mid-1970s, and Sweden was still sterilising transgender people as a condition for their being entitled to state-sponsored surgery up until 2012.

Next came Sweden's classification of HIV/AIDS under Sweden's existing communicable disease legislation (for example see Baldwin 2005; Danziger 1999; Fox et al. 1989; Kirp and Bayer 1992; Kulick 2003; Kulick 2005; Vallgårda 2007), most recently revised in the 1960s, just after the height of Sweden's mass sterilisations. Unlike other European states, who arguably decided to move away from those more repressive techniques that had been favoured in the 19th and early 20th centuries in their HIV prevention and treatment intervention – focussing on techniques of 'cooperation and inclusion' instead – Sweden's strategy was to continue in its projects of 'containment and control' of groups perceived to pose a risk of transmitting the infection (Kirp and Bayer 1992) and thus who were seen to pose a risk to the health of the normatively acceptable populations of the People's Home. As stressed above, Sweden's contagious disease legislation allowed, and still does allow, for compulsory testing, treatment, and potentially indefinite compulsory medicalised incarceration for those who are perceived to be recalcitrant and/or unable to follow physicians' instructions. This includes those who do not disclose their HIV status before activities seen to pose the risk of transmission, including all types of sexual intercourse. Those who do not cooperate with compulsory contact tracing, and/or do not attend medical testing and inspection when summoned following identification during contact tracing may well have to contend with the unannounced arrival and escort of the Swedish police (indeed, there was media coverage of just such an incident during the time I lived in Sweden).

And as with venereal disease and vagrancy legislation, as well as eugenic projects and sterilisations discussed above, the implementation of the communicable disease legislation as policy has not been symmetrical: as with Sweden's historical legislation, Sweden's HIV/AIDS communicable disease legislation was in fact a lens through which to focus on communities who were/are constructed as posing a threat to normative social order, a threat to Sweden's efforts to socially engineer a rational, moral, and modern 'People's Home'. Thus, those who came to be subject to the state's repressive and paternalistic gaze were people who use drugs, gay men, and sex workers; all of these groups were seen to pose a risk of transmission of HIV from deviant and subversive populations to the normative population, to pose yet another threat to the stability of the homogeneous and clean *folkhemmet.* These groups are amongst those that have historically been constructed in Sweden as eugenically deficient and unable to conduct themselves appropriately and exercise due agency and self-control (Harrington 2012); they are regarded as being in need of imposed control and care, both for their own good and for the good of Swedish society at large. And so, come the early 1990s, all of those living with HIV who had been compulsorily isolated were drug users and sex workers, some of whom were locked away without the prospect of release for years (indeed, some died in medicalised incarceration) (Henriksson and Ytterberg 1992). At a time when much of Europe was arguably embracing a move towards a more inclusive *post*modernity, with a queering of normative, delineated, and binary expectations, Sweden effectively (re)affirmed its commitment to modernity, to rationalisation, to social engineering, and to regimented and aggressively delineated social construction (and social exclusion, and control). As one respondent, from the Swedish Institute for Communicable Disease Control, noted: 'people that are actually taken into care or custody or whatever, are always the weaker groups, although theoretically it could be anyone. But in practice it will always be weaker groups in society.'

And these social controls that have typified Sweden's legislation and policy are widely accepted by Swedish citizens. As will become clear, particularly in the following two chapters, the Swedish state has been able to achieve a great consensus – both politically and in civil society – on radically repressive action being taken in the context of what are frequently divisive topics in other states. This may be attributed to the strong sense of social responsibility that is felt by a great many Swedes, an acceptance and support of the Swedish nation state that attends Sweden's rational projects of modernity (Gould 2005; Henriksson and Ytterberg 1992).

Methodology

The foci of my research

I was only partially aware of Sweden's history of violent social engineering when I moved to Stockholm in 2008 to conduct research for the purposes of my PhD at the University of Cambridge, from which this book stems. During my three and a half year residence and research in Sweden, which was funded by the UK ESRC (Economic and Social Research Council), the extent of the social exclusion of marginalised communities in Sweden became startlingly apparent to me.

The original focus of my doctoral research was on the outcomes of the Swedish *sexköpslagen*, 'the sex purchase law' which criminalised the purchase of sex in 1999 and which has been hugely internationally influential and divisive.[6] What made Sweden's legislation on sex work unique at the time is that it focusses on *demand*; the case is the same with Sweden's criminalisation of people who use drugs: those who *use* drugs, and those who *buy* sex, are criminalised. In terms of Sweden's sex work legislation, the introduction of the *sexköpslagen* served to set Sweden apart from other countries, whilst simultaneously aligning Sweden's engagement with two of its most marginalised communities through this concentration on demand (Gould 2001).

Commonalities in how people who use drugs and sex workers have come to be understood and treated in Sweden do not end with a legislative focus on demand.[7] Though my research began with a specific concentration on an exploration of the outcomes of the 1999 sex purchase law, as fieldwork and interviews continued, alliances between sex work and drug use activist organisations in Sweden became increasingly clear and pertinent to my research. Indeed, issues surrounding drug use came to ground my understanding of sex work in terms of broader social exclusions, social controls, stigma and discrimination, and containment and control.

During the course of fieldwork, people who use drugs and sex workers, as well as advocacy and rights organisations, reported similarities between their respective communities' experiences and difficulties with service and healthcare providers, with the authorities and the police and Swedish security forces, as well as noting similar issues in the context of meaningful inclusion and contribution (or lack thereof) of people who use drugs and sex workers to political debate and evaluation pertaining to those respective groups. In short, it became apparent during my research on the outcomes of the *sexköpslagen* that I could study neither sex work nor drug use in Sweden in isolation: Sweden's projects of social control and social engineering are broader in scope than a focus on only one community, as I hope to have made clear above. Indeed, it would have been remiss of me to omit either from my fieldwork and research, and it would have been remiss of me to publish only my findings on the outcomes of Sweden's sex work legislation – hence the importance of this book. Similarities and parallels in experiences of people who use drugs and of sex workers in Sweden serve to illustrate broader projects of discipline and social engineering, and they reflect commonalities in difficulties, dangers, and impacts on health and welfare that have resulted from repressive and criminalising legislation, as I have emphasised in this chapter, and will explore during the following chapters.[8]

Moving into the People's Home

My first trip to Sweden was in 2008, and involved pilot fieldwork preceding my PhD research, ascertaining the feasibility of fieldwork and research and meeting with key respondents and organisations prior to my moving to live in the country later the same year. I lived in various areas of Stockholm over a period of three and a half years, and also conducted research in Malmo.

Meeting respondents

As a result of their being criminalised and socially excluded in many contexts, people who use drugs make up an extremely clandestine community. Indeed, people who use drugs often have to remain invisible – or at least keep their drug use invisible – in order to survive (both figuratively, and sometimes literally). Thus, no clear and delineated sampling frame was available for the purposes of my research (and the same applied to my fieldwork investigating the outcomes of Sweden's sex work legislation) (Heckathorn 1997). My methodological approach thus called for methods of triangulation, that is, the use of several varying approaches collectively and in harmony (Jick 1979), where looking from different perspectives and angles allows for a greater clarity of perception, for greater and clearer understanding of complex societal issues. Triangulation allowed for the limitations of some methodological approaches to be offset by other approaches, at least to some extent (no method is without its limitations!). Triangulation also allowed for the validation/corroboration of respondent testimony, with respondents of varying backgrounds collectively contributing to a holistic picture of drug policy and law and their outcomes in and on Swedish society. I gathered a breadth of ethnographic data (Atkinson and Hammersley 1994; Becker 1958), principally through participant observation and qualitative interviews with respondents. In terms of sampling respondents, I used several methods, none without its drawbacks, but all with distinct positives that supplemented and augmented one another. From the outset, it became clear that some sampling methods, such as respondent-driven sampling (Abdul-Quader et al. 2006), would be impossible, since the fact that many respondents were so isolated from other members of their community meant that relying on their networks to recruit further respondents would not have produced sufficiently large samples, even for the purposes of gathering indicative anecdotal testimony (Heckathorn 1997; Simic et al. 2006). Respondents were therefore sampled using numerous sampling methods, which collectively mitigated the limitations presented by all modes of sampling of hidden and clandestine populations. Respondents were accessed through key informant sampling; targeted sampling; and snowball sampling.

Key informant sampling allowed me to build up a broad understanding of wider debates, discourses, and the evolution and genealogy of Swedish drug policy. Through an exploration of secondary literature, and through early interviews, I was able to establish which key organisations and stakeholders would be of particular relevance to the focus of my work (Tammi 2005a). Though these respondents did not necessarily have personal experiences of drug use in Sweden, approaching these key informants, key organisations, and interviewing these organisations' representatives allowed me to build up a picture of the broad context of Sweden's drug legislation and policy, and also allowed me to snowball further respondents for interview, where key respondents would refer me on to their contacts, and those on to theirs, and so forth. Snowball sampling was particularly useful given the foci of my fieldwork, where though respondent-driven sampling was not possible, snowballing respondents allowed me to make use of respondents' networks where they were available, however limited they were. This is a key mode of contact in situations where respondents/the phenomenon of study is obscure, criminalised, concealed, and/or clandestine (Başoğlu 1997; Heckathorn et al. 2002; Jorgensen 1989; Kurtz et al. 2005; Noy 2008; Scambler et al. 1990), as was the case here.

Other respondents were accessed via a combination of targeted sampling and targeted convenience sampling, in which people who use drugs and those who contribute to drug policy discourse and debate were met in public spaces and/or through relevant organisations and networks; this allowed for respondents with direct experience of drug use in Sweden to be met, respondents who might have been excluded through key informant sampling (Watters and Biernacki 1989). Relationships were fostered with many of these individuals and networks over time and indeed I am still in contact with several of these networks years after the research. These sampling methods were coupled with further snowball sampling and extensive participant observation, with time spent at networks observing the day-to-day workings of individuals, activists, and organisations. These observations, though sporadic, took place over several years and/or for the entire duration of the research (Becker and Geer 1957; Burgess 1981; Stacey 1988), and provided an essential context to the more formal interviews that I conducted. There were no distinct boundaries between my social time and my research when living in Sweden, and I kept a password-protected field diary to make regular notes of my participant observation and developments in my fieldwork and research.

As I have reflected elsewhere, as a non-Swedish national I often felt like an outsider on the inside of Swedish society (Levy 2015; also see Pred 2000); however, it bears repeating that I spent extensive amounts of time with many respondents, I met many respondents as a result of relationships I had forged with their contacts, colleagues, and friends, and prior to undertaking this research I already knew people and communities of people who use(d) drugs, as well as other groups who were pertinent to my fieldwork and research (specifically sex workers, LGBTQ people and communities, workers and activists in the field of HIV). I therefore feel that my association and participation with various queer (and 'deviant') communities, not to mention the fact that my personal interests and political perspectives had come to influence my work and, circularly, been influenced by it (Pyett 2003), resulted (and result) in my identity being queered to some extent. My academic 'heteronormal prudery' (Hubbard 1999) was less of an impediment than it perhaps may have been. That is not to say that my positionality did not require considerable reflexivity (see Levy 2015), only that in some instances I was positioned as an insider on the outside of Swedish normatively acceptable society (Ahmed 2011), not solely the converse.

Interviews, consent, and confidentiality

Interviews were semi-structured, open ended, and qualitative, and followed the course of key themes that were chosen prior to (and inductively developed during) interview based on each respondents' expertise and lived experience. They were essentially guided, themed conversations, with respondents free to pause and discontinue interview at any point. Transcriptions (which I undertook myself) from the research which informs this book, came to over 400,000 words. I explained the nature of my research and foci to respondents prior to interview, so they were aware that participation was voluntary (Homan 2001), and their informed consent was obtained orally (Des Jarlais et al. 1999; Sachs et al. 2003). Interviews were conducted in safe spaces that would be free from interruption (Day and Topp 2003; Elwood and Martin 2000; Zimmerman and Watts 2003). Interviews were conducted in respondents' homes, in restaurants, bars, cafés, and the offices of organisations and rights organisations, with the last of these in particular offering safe interview environments (Day and Topp 2003). Where respondents were told that they would be recorded, and gave their informed consent for this, they were assured that if I quoted their testimony, or referred to anything they had said, this would be anonymous. Though I undertook intensive Swedish language training, which proved useful in assisting during interviews with colloquialisms and some terminology and vernacular, the vast majority of respondents spoke excellent English and interviews were generally conducted in English without difficulty.

Anonymity of respondents was very important, given both the sensitivity of much of what we were to discuss during interview, and the fact that being outed as a drug user, or even as someone who works with communities of people who use drugs and with other criminalised and stigmatised communities, can result in negative repercussions, social exclusion, police involvement, and violence and risks to health and safety (Cwikel and Hoban 2005; Ellsberg and Heise 2002; Shaver 2005; WHO 2001). Transcriptions were anonymised, and respondents were named for my records only in an encrypted spreadsheet, kept separate from interview transcriptions which were, in turn, password protected.

Presentation of research

Transcribed interviews were analysed according to Grounded Theory (Glaser and Strauss 1967), where the themes emergent during interviews informed key sections of my write up, thus informing the structure and coverage of this book. Interview transcripts were thematically coded both during and following transcription along the lines of emergent themes (and subthemes); the creation of new themes, with corresponding headings and subheadings, ceased when no new topics emerged from interviews, when thematic 'saturation' was reached. Once all interviews were analysed, pertinent respondent testimony had been (re)organised in a structure that could be arranged and rearranged until a satisfactory flow to the narrative of this book had been achieved.

People who use drugs are often positioned as passive, both in research and, indeed, in debates surrounding the formation of policy and law. Where possible, therefore, I quote respondents directly, emphasising a respect for respondents as experts on their own lives and lived experiences (Wahab 2003). Processes of interview transcription, coding, and resultant (re)organisation has allowed for a presentation of respondents' testimony in a manner designed to facilitate testimony 'speaking' for itself; the processes have also enabled the inclusion of substantial and variable respondent quotations related to the topics discussed in the following chapters. I have endeavoured to include quotations of numerous respondents simultaneously, presenting them side-by-side. This not only actively positions respondents' testimony in the midst of my discussions, but additionally lets respondents' testimony direct and inform the flow and nature of my discussions and arguments; my own prose essentially serves to frame the narratives, views, and arguments posited by respondents. In addition, this presentation of quotations from numerous respondents concurrently allows for their juxtaposition, addressing themes and opinions from different perspectives – but on the same topic – simultaneously, side-by-side. As I have noted (and quoted) elsewhere (Levy 2015), and as in Pred's seminal study of Swedish discourses of social engineering, eugenics, migration, and racisms, *Even in Sweden* (2000: xiii), 'I have intermingled my own voice with very differently situated voices that speak past one another as often as they speak to one another… juxtaposing the incompatible and the contradictory… a multilayered mode of expression'. Selection of which quotations to include was not simple, but I have, where possible, included the voices of those actors who are most illustratively apposite to various discussions, also taking into account aesthetics, form, flow, and ethics (Sandelowski 1994).

Where I quote a respondent's testimony, I refer to their relevant organisational affiliation (including previous affiliation where pertinent), as well as how they identify in the context of their interview (for example, if they identify as a drug user, as a former drug user, and so forth). Where more than one person representing the same organisation was interviewed, I have ensured that their references are differentiated so as to allow the reader to tell their testimony apart.

A brief (but important) note on language

Language is very important when writing on themes of criminalisation, social exclusion, violence, stigma and discrimination, and activities and/or phenomena which have come to galvanise moral panics[9] and social (re)constructions that serve to marginalise and demonise communities. Simply positioning respondents as active in my discussions is not sufficient: the words and terms I use to refer to communities and activities must also be carefully considered. For example, problematic terms which relate to people who use drugs (and to the drugs they use) include 'junkie', 'crackhead', 'druggie', 'speed freak', 'dope fiend' and so forth; to downplay the power and implications of such language, of such pejorative words and terms, is to deny very real signification that serves to subjugate, denigrate, other, and marginalise people who use drugs. Even taken-for-granted terms that are commonly used, which may appear superficially benign, deserve our attention. To be said to be 'clean', for instance, as well as connoting 'drug-free' (or, in the case of blood-borne and sexually transmitted infections like HIV, 'infection-free') also implies that to occupy the opposite position in this binary – in this case, to be an active drug user – is to be conversely 'dirty', and thus to be 'of less worth and, as such, [these terms] can denigrate and marginalise' (INPUD 2011); similarly, as Keane (2002: 18) has aptly noted in her analysis of the social construction of addiction, even the seemingly inert 'words "chemical" and "substance" cannot be used to avoid the morally and politically loaded cultural category of drugs. The term "chemical" has its own powerful negative connotations, particularly when juxtaposed with a notion of the body as organic and natural.'

Additionally, due to their connotation and implication, the terms 'addict' and 'addiction' are argued to be 'pejorative and stigmatising' (Larkin et al. 2006: 207–208).[10] The construction of the diseased 'addict' or 'drug abuser' (see INPUD 2011) with a 'pathological relationship between the subject and the substance' (Keane 2002: 37), the addict assumed as a 'sick person', should, it is argued, give way to a more neutral idea of a 'drug user' (Stimson 1989), or 'people who use drugs' (INPUD 2011). As will be discussed in Chapter 2, the World Health Organization recommended about fifty years ago that the terms 'addiction' and 'addict' be abandoned, using instead drug 'dependence', to depend on a drug in various situations, or to get through the day.

Terminology should be contested and used carefully, addressing reductionist and derogatory assumptions and not simply assuming terms to be neutral, impassive, and unproblematic simply because they are commonly used (Larkin et al. 2006). Favoured terms and understandings will, no doubt, continue to transform and transmute over time; what is imperative, though, is that understanding and assumption should be broken down, deconstructed, and contested. Terminology and discourse are, as I have been at pains to emphasise, enormously powerful. My choice of terminology, of metaphor, of construction, should therefore not be a blasé or simplistically accepting one.

Overview of this book

This book begins with an exploration of how Sweden came to legislate so radically in 1988, moving from analyses of political debates to analyses of social (re)constructions and understandings.

This Introduction has outlined Sweden's history of socially and spatially controlling and containing various marginalised groups, with an aim of socially engineering a homogeneous, rational, and modern *folkhemmet,* and has illustrated Sweden's history of social control through a brief summary of Sweden's treatment of marginalised groups through the 19th and 20th centuries – namely LGBT people, women, sex workers, and people with drug and alcohol dependencies. Chapter 1 then focusses on the mood in Sweden prior to and during the introduction of Sweden's contemporary prohibitionist drug laws. I argue that in-migration of considerable numbers of people, coupled with concern, blame, and stigma surrounding the HIV/AIDS pandemic in the 1980s, resulted in a revival of historical concerns surrounding the identity and homogeneity of the Swedish nation state, galvanising moral panics relating to drug use, as well as what were/are perceived to be alien drugs and patterns of drug use. I emphasise in this first chapter that it was these panics, which were provoked and exacerbated by various political and civil society groups in the 1970s and 1980s, which resulted in the criminalisation of the use of drugs in Sweden and the introduction of legislation allowing for the compulsory treatment of those with drug dependencies.

Chapter 2 discusses the social constructions of people who use drugs in Sweden – and the understandings of drugs themselves – that provide a discursive backdrop that serves to justify Swedish prohibitionist rhetoric, legislation, and policy. This chapter emphasises that much of this social construction stems from an 'addiction-as-disease' model of understanding, which casts people who use drugs and people with drug dependencies as simultaneously sick and infantilised, whilst being additionally dangerous, deviant, and criminal. Augmenting this model of understanding is a peculiarly Swedish perception of drug use *itself* as a disease, spread from individual to individual by people who use drugs. The chapter critiques and deconstructs these models of understanding, arguing that they are used to undermine the agency and self-determination of people who use drugs, feeding through into their being controlled, criminalised (as discussed in the previous chapter), and denied access to service and healthcare provision (discussed further in Chapter 4). This chapter additionally unpacks the Swedish understandings of drugs that have followed through into legislation and dominant discourse. It will explore what are perceived to be culturally Swedish, normative drugs, with a focus on alcohol and Swedish 'snus' oral tobaccos, and the associations these have with Swedish heteronormative masculinity. It also discusses what are seen to be alien, foreign, deviant drugs, with these perceptions fed by xenophobia and racisms.

Chapter 3 discusses levels and spaces of drug use in Sweden. Advocates of the Swedish model of drug prohibition argue that criminalisation of people who use drugs is imperative in reducing drug use, and this chapter demonstrates that, historically, levels of drug use in Sweden have been low, and it explores whether there is evidence that the prohibitionist legislation introduced in the 1980s has been responsible for any decline, or a maintenance of relatively low levels, of drug use. Having discussed levels of drug use in Sweden, the chapter then explores Sweden's 'public drug scenes' – public areas where drugs are bought and sold – with Stockholm providing an involved case study. It is argued that Sweden's criminalising legislation has been used selectively as a tool with which to displace the unwanted nuisance of people who use drugs from public space; parallels are drawn with the Swedish criminalisation of the purchase of sex, which has similarly been used selectively to police and sanitise public space through a selective enforcement of the criminalisation of demand.

Chapter 4 explores service provision and harm reduction interventions for people who use drugs, both in Sweden and, for comparative purposes, to some extent internationally. The chapter begins with an overview of what harm reduction involves, and why harm reduction is imperative if the human rights and health of people who use drugs are to be prioritised. Discussion then moves on to the opposition that many Swedish policy makers and service providers have to harm reduction interventions for people who use drugs.

The chapter then explores which services are (and, more pressingly, are not) available for people who use drugs in Sweden, discussing why some services are opposed and to what extent they are seen to be (mis)aligned with Sweden's drug legislation and discourse. Chapter 5 very much follows on from the preceding chapter, with an exploration of the experiences of people who use drugs of Swedish service provision and service providers. Key themes include conditionality of service provision, punitive and controlling interactions, disempowering and disciplining of people who use drugs who access service provision, infantilisation, social exclusion, and structural violence.

Chapter 6 describes the on-the-ground outcomes of Swedish prohibitionist drugs legislation and policy, as well as the results of the understandings and discourses that inform these laws and policies on the lives and experiences of people who use drugs in Sweden. It principally focusses on demonstrating the impacts that Swedish prohibitionism has had on the wellbeing and health of people who use drugs. The chapter then discusses the effects of social exclusion and a lack of holistic service provision, which has resulted in one of the highest overdose mortality rates in Europe, with people who use drugs being disincentivised to contact healthcare and service providers when they are needed due to their being criminalised. The chapter focuses heavily on the actions of the Swedish police and security forces, who perpetrate systemic and endemic state-sponsored abuse and violence against people who use drugs.

The Conclusion of the book summarises my findings, and addresses Sweden's positioning itself as a progressive beacon for other states to follow. It sets out the true outcomes of criminalisation, discrimination, and stigmatisation of people who use drugs. Sweden's efforts to internationally export various 'Swedish models' on what are constructed as unwanted social 'nuisances' will be discussed. Whilst calling into question the legitimacy of Sweden's international posturing, the Conclusion also reemphasises the myopia of engaging only with Sweden's current policies pertaining to individual communities, activities, and/or phenomena, stressing the importance of examining these in the context of Sweden's history of modernity, social control and social engineering.

Notes

1 Laws and these social constructions themselves hold what are a myriad and diverse group of substances together under the label of what I here refer to as 'drugs'. The term 'drug', used to connote various psychoactive, stimulant, and depressant substances, is a relatively recent one, used in this context predominantly through the 20th century (see Seddon 2010). It should be clear, though, that for the purposes of this book, I take 'drugs' and 'drug use' to refer to the non-medically sanctioned use of drugs, whether the substance(s) in question is/are criminalised, controlled, or prescription.

2 Though I must emphasise that definitions of 'discourse' are multiple and divergent, I use discourse in this book along Foucauldian lines (Foucault 1981; also see, for example, Lennie et al. 2003; Levy 2015; Pennycook 1994) in reference to modes of establishing and constituting knowledge(s). A discourse, in this context, should be understood as a broad set of ideas pertaining to a 'thing', 'phenomenon', and/or 'construct(s)', with sets of ideas and themes consolidated and concretised as a Discourse of/on whatever the aforementioned 'thing' may be (in the context of this book, 'addiction discourse' would be one such example). Discourses can be promoted and disseminated by various

institutions (for example schools, religious institutions, prisons, hospitals, and, in the case of this particular book, service and healthcare providers targeting people who use drugs), and this informs their becoming dominant discourses in society, that is discourses that dominate the popular imagination. This has a lot to do with how various phenomena, behaviours, and identities come to be socially constructed and defined, and then pass as the 'real', as 'natural', timeless and True, despite their being socially constructed discourses. Thus, it is necessary to deconstruct discourses to reveal how they are constructed in the first place. Dominant discourse directly informs what comes to be understood as normative and normatively acceptable, as well as what is conversely defined as deviant, as threatening normative social order (discussed in a below note). Thus, some discourses are undermined, sidelined, and invisiblised, whilst dominant discourses render themselves as fact. Sexuality, race, and gender are all notable examples of discourses that pass for 'natural', timeless, and 'true', yet are, as Foucault and others have insisted, socially constructed discourses; they are *produced* (Butler 2004; Howell 2007; Keane 2002; Wilchins 2004). This book will be concerned with social constructions and discourses pertaining to people who use drugs and of drugs themselves, as well as discourses of addiction, disease, and drug policy.

3 For these purposes, 'liberal' should be taken, according to a more 'layperson' understanding, to mean a prioritisation of individual liberties and 'freedoms', with the governing of the state distinguished from a 'sphere of individual liberty' (Dean 2002: 37). A liberal state therefore prioritises and respects the self-determination and agency of individuals in civil society. It should be stressed, however, that in so-called 'liberal' societies 'advanced liberal' processes of governance can involve practices and policies which may be understood as somewhat authoritarian and repressive, essentially (and paradoxically) as 'illiberal'. These 'advanced liberal authoritarian techniques' (Harrington 2012) are not, therefore, mutually exclusive from a liberal society. But, to reiterate, I use the term 'liberal' according to its common usage.

4 *Lagom*, arguably a quintessentially Swedish notion, does not translate well into English! It may translate crudely as 'just the right amount of' or 'a perfect balance/compromise of' or 'an appropriate/suitable level of'. My apologies to any Swedish readers for the crudity of my attempts at translating this untranslatable term, but rest assured that I consulted with several Swedish friends.

5 'Normative', as with 'discourse' is used in this book along Foucauldian lines (Foucault 1976; Foucault 1979). It should be taken to connote the socially normal and acceptable. These norms come to be promoted and accepted, and can pertain to community, identity, drug use, sexuality, work, race and ethnicity, for example. This contrasts with 'deviant', which connotes communities, identities, behaviours, and so forth, that are constructed as posing a threat to normative social order and normative discourse, something which deviates from socially constructed moral acceptability. Ideas and discourses of normativity and deviance are liable to be reimagined when dominant discourses shift and transmogrify.

6 My research on the outcomes of the Swedish criminalisation of the purchase of sex is presented in full in *Criminalising the Purchase of Sex: Lessons from Sweden* (Levy 2015)

7 It should be stressed that where there may be crossovers and intersections between sex work and drug use, universalising people who sell sex as people who use drugs, or vice versa, would be misleading and simplistic. People who use drugs and people who sell sex should not be conflated or generalised. Though high levels of drug use are noted amongst female *street* sex workers, 'high levels of drug use… are not found in studies of indoor sex work markets' (Cusick et al. 2009: 707; also see Spice 2007). Furthermore, causality between sex work and drug use, where one activity is undertaken due to the other, should not be generalised or assumed.

8 Though this book focusses on Sweden's criminalisation of the use of drugs and the outcomes of that criminalisation on the lived realities of people who use drugs and the dynamics of drug use in Sweden, my research on sex work legislation will not fall by

the wayside during these discussions; elements of that research are pertinent to my explorations and analyses of Swedish drug law and policy. This is notably the case in the context of discussions of legislation being used as a lens through which to police, sanitise, and moralise public space, to displace people who use drugs (and sex workers) from civil society; discussion of these two communities is also of relevance in terms of discussions of service and healthcare provision and harm reduction interventions.

9 'Moral panics' should be taken to be phenomena where the (ostensible) concern(s) in question is/are seen to pose an escalating, pressing, and *deviant* threat to *normative* social order and structure (with 'moral panic' as a phrase famously coined by Cohen [1972]).

10 I ascribe to the view of 'addict' and 'addiction' being problematic, pejorative, and unhelpful terms; the addiction-as-disease model of understanding is discussed in greater detail in Chapter 2 of this book.

1 Historical, legal, discursive precedent

This chapter is principally an historical genealogy of the political debates that immediately preceded, and resulted in, the introduction of Sweden's 1988 legislation criminalising the use of drugs and allowing for medicalised detention and forced treatment of those with drug dependencies. Sweden's 1988 legislation resulted in people who use drugs being directly criminalised, as opposed to being criminalised indirectly through legislation criminalising possession, supply, and other activities *surrounding* drug use. I focus here also on how these debates, both those which occurred in government and those which took place in the media, came to redefine how drugs and people who use them were viewed in Sweden; this redefining came to inform the view that compulsory medicalised detention for people with drug dependencies was imperative.

I begin by discussing the context in which the debates took place. Concern surrounding drug use in the 20th century in Sweden was by no means in a vacuum, and I focus on various moral panics that set the stage for an increase in popular and political concern surrounding not just drugs, but what drugs came to represent for Sweden: an alien threat to the normative, rational, disciplined *folkhemmet.* I concentrate on how criminalising the use of drugs, and legislating to allow for compulsory care for people with drug dependencies came to be seen as essential steps to be taken in Sweden's pursuit of a drug-free society, and in so doing I focus on which groups and stakeholders were instrumental in the debates surrounding the topic. I focus also on which groups came to be sidelined and silenced, and how.

Moral panic in the People's Home: racism, HIV/AIDS, and drugs

> '[It is] not surprising that irrational and exaggerated fears have grown up about immigrants, drugs and perhaps – the international sex trade'.
>
> (Gould 2001: 453)

Within Sweden, Swedish people are felt to have a long tradition of drug use. Indeed, one respondent with the Swedish police emphasised that 'the rage of the Vikings came from the beer and [psychoactive] substance with[in] mushrooms' (Interview, Stockholm Police [Narcotics Division Team Leader]; also see

Boekhout van Solinge 1997). Alcohol use is seen to be inherent to Swedishness, with the acceptable use of alcohol in Sweden marked by binge drinking and its use as a psychoactive drug (drinking to get drunk), as opposed to moderate drinking patterns found elsewhere in Europe (discussed further in the following chapters); indeed, Swedish people are not felt (and often do not feel) to be capable of moderating their intake of alcohol and other substances (Van der Giessen and Van Brussel 1996). Further, levels of non-alcoholic substance use dramatically increased in the 1950s and 1960s, when prescription of opiates and amphetamines 'went totally out of control' (Van der Giessen and Van Brussel 1996; also see Lenke and Olsson 2002; Lindberg and Haynes 2000; UNODC 2006). High levels of diversion/leakage of prescription drugs to the illicit market compounded concerns in Sweden as to the rise of the use of untraditional and 'un-Swedish drugs', feeding into worries regarding drug spread and foreign practices and patterns of drug use.

> 'There was an era of hedonism, Sweden is a part of the world, of course, like any other nation, and anybody who lived in the sixties, I did, I was a teenager then... it was a time when it was very cool to be liberal, have a liberal attitude towards drugs'.
>
> (Interview, RNS)

> 'What happened in the late fifties and early sixties, in Sweden, it was like we had an explosion of drugs... pills that they used to lose weight... It got a whole generation addicted to these types... of substance, and we also of course had, we had cannabis, we had, in the middle of the sixties and late sixties we had a huge problem in Sweden with heroin'.
>
> (Interview, Stockholm Police [Narcotics Division Team Leader])

> 'During the sixties in Sweden, we had a period for like 10, 15, 20 years when we were very liberal in Sweden... we had these legal prescription programmes. Any doctor could prescribe any drug of choice. But it was no programme or no regulation... then it turned into become this repressive, restrictive drug policy that we still have'.
>
> (Interview, Chair and Founder of *Svenska Brukarföreningen*)

Although this 'explosion of drugs' was arguably an hyperbole unjustified by the real situation (Hallam 2010), it seems to have precipitated a broader moral panic in Sweden (Boekhout van Solinge 1997). Statistics illustrating stabilising or decreasing drug use were claimed to be misleading (Gould 1989; also see Boekhout van Solinge 1997), and focus was not on statistics or evidence *per se*, but on emotive and ideological assertions, on the implications of the use of certain drugs and on who was associated with these drugs. It is not surprising that declarations of Stockholm being 'awash with amphetamines' (Gould 1989) caused alarm, with the visibility of public drug scenes, perceived as corrupting and polluting the clean and orderly *folkhemmet*, resulting in further concern.

> 'In the eighties and the nineties, it was a very big population in T-Centralen [Stockholm's central subway station]... a very open selling, and so they had to do something'.
>
> (Interview, KRIS)

Concerns surrounding drugs were coupled with a fear of the foreign[1] (Gould 1996; Hallam 2010): foreign drugs, foreign practices, foreign people, foreign cultures; all of these fears intersected with Sweden's relative geographical and political isolation and with Sweden's historical efforts to maintain an ordered *folkhemmet.* Panic surrounding drug use was racialised and xenophobically associated with Sweden's rapidly increasing migrant populace (see Pred 2000), with immigrants and foreign states seen to be the cause of the inflow of new and dangerous substances and practices (Gould 1996; Gould 2001).

> 'We are a little corner, way up north, in Sweden; we have been a society with very little influence from the outside. So when narcotics came to Sweden, when drugs came to Sweden, it scared a lot, I mean "what is this? What is happening to our youth, what is happening to", you know, the same old moral panic.'
>
> (Interview, Chair of RFHL)

Swedish fear of foreign substances (and peoples) was compounded by concerns surrounding economic instability during the 1970s (Lenke and Olsson 2002) and furthermore a fear of the newly erupting HIV/AIDS pandemic and concern about its spread to the normative population from and by groups constructed to be deviant and dangerous. People who use drugs were rendered as dangerously unpredictable, with racialised generalisations informing racist stereotypes of hypersexualised, alien drug users, 'whose unpredictable lifestyle hindered compliance' with HIV testing and prevention interventions (Baldwin 2005: 76; also see Månsson et al. 2000; Tammi 2005b; Vallgårda 2007). The crude conflations of these fears and panics in the media and in state-run information campaigns drew on Swedish racist and xenophobic discourse, no doubt fed by Sweden's history of eugenically informed social construction and engineering; these were narratives of drug using, foreign people of colour infecting Swedes, both at home and abroad (Henriksson and Ytterberg 1992).

Legislation came at a time when drug use – and all it was associated with – seemed to threaten to undermine an orderly, safe, homogeneous *folkhemmet.* Several narratives fed through into legislation and its discursive justifications, all with a backdrop of a 'successfully socially constructed' drug issue (Lenke and Olsson 2002: 67). It was far from difficult in Sweden to scapegoat and problematise people who use drugs and those with dependencies as necessitating control in such a climate of instability and fear (Gould 1989), especially in the context of Sweden's history of problematising, containing, and controlling such communities.

The commissions and *remiss* responses: creating a drug-free society

Swedish parliament noted the arguably unachievable and utopian ambition to achieve a 'drug-free society' in 1977 (Anker 2007) and a 1984 bill explicitly detailed this aim (UNODC 2006); indeed, during the legal debate and campaigns that led up to legislation, there were constant references to the aspiration for a 'drug-free society'.

In 1988 Sweden criminalised the use of drugs, it becoming a criminal offence to have drugs in one's bloodstream. This was coupled with a widening of existing LVM (*lagen om vård av missbrukare* ['The Law for the Care of Misusers/Abusers']) legislation, allowing for the compulsory treatment of those with drug and alcohol dependencies. The expanded LVM legislation is perhaps consistent and unsurprising given Sweden's history of control, prohibition, and temperance (Anker 2007; Gould 1989; Lindberg and Haynes 2000), and can be seen as an outcome of an historical 'cultural desire for order' (Gould 1989: 731), a social order that has been achieved through strikingly violent and invasive means, as described in this book's Introduction. Sweden's prohibitionist laws on drug use are focussed primarily on three areas: reducing the number of people commencing drug use, encouraging people who use drugs to cease drug use, and reducing the supply of drugs (EMCDDA 2010; Hallam 2010).

The criminalisation of the use of drugs and the introduction of (renewable) six months compulsory care for those with dependencies were preceded by two government commissioned reports that went out on *remiss* consultation. Sweden's *remiss* consultations are the process through which numerous parties may contribute to political debate and discussion that results in legislative change. Initially, the government will commission a Commission investigation, which investigates the issue in question and is then published; it is at this point that interested parties, stakeholders, and organisations can then respond to the report and to proposals with their views, criticisms, and suggestions and/or demands. Following this, a Bill is drawn up, which is then subject to parliamentary vote, and legislation is then passed (or not). It is to these commissioned reports and *remiss* consultations that I now turn my attention:

Criminalising use

Swedish governments have historically opposed criminalising the use of drugs, considering it to be out of keeping with traditional policy not to legislate against something that affects only the individual, not broader society (Gould 1989).[2] From 1982, political opposition (to the governing Social Democratic Party) had annually raised the issue of criminalising the use of drugs, with key governmental figures also supporting a tougher approach to drugs and drug users (Gould 1989). Having regained power in the early 1980s, the Social Democrats launched a *remiss* Commission report which proposed a slight strengthening of the penal law but importantly did *not* recommend criminalising the use of drugs, as was being demanded by opposition parties (Gould 1989). Criticism and protests resulted from political opposition and NGOs (Lenke and Olsson 2002), the latter of which is discussed further below. Some concern was expressed during the *remiss* consultation that a criminalisation of the use of drugs would push the perceived problem of drug use underground, exacerbating difficulties and dangers for people who use drugs; but following the *remiss* consultation a proposal to criminalise the use of drugs was reviewed by parliament. It was argued that 'the overall effect would be to maximize the possibility of people who used drugs giving up the habit or seeking help and support' (Gould 1989: 733).

The best way to tackle perceived influxes of dangerous substances, therefore, was seen to be to focus on the consumer, on demand for drugs (Anker 2007; Gould 1989; Gould 2001), a focus notably advocated by the founder of a prohibitionist Swedish NGO called RNS (*riksförbundet Narkotikafritt Samhälle* ['Association for a Drug-Free Society']), Nils Bejerot (discussed further below), who believed that 'the drug user was the irreplaceable element in the drug chain' (UNODC 2006: 13). It was ambitiously asserted by RNS that once demand was undermined and eliminated, the whole 'drugs pyramid' would simply collapse:

> '*narkotika pyramiden* [the drugs pyramid], our policy is based on this idea that without the base, which is the consumers, we wouldn't have a problem and... our policy is based upon this... If there are buyers they will, there will always be sellers'.
>
> (Interview, IOGT-NTO; previously RNS)

> 'As long as there's a market, you can never stop the supply of drugs. The drugs will always be there. But if the consumers, if the need for drugs decreased, the amount of drugs will decrease. Simple market economy.'
>
> (Interview, Stockholm Police [Narcotics Division Team Leader])

> 'Their perspective is always more repressive, if you take away the people on the street, you don't have any problem with drugs. So put them into jail, put them into custody, put them into the forests of northern Sweden, and there they can be. And if you take it away, the drug dealers will disappear.'
>
> (Interview, RFHL)

> 'The aim of Swedish drug policy is to achieve a drug-free society; drug users are said to be controlled by their drugs and may need compulsory care and treatment to free them of their addiction; policy measures focus upon consumers, since without them, there would be no market; abstention is the goal of treatment; and there is a concern about drugs flooding into the country from overseas.'
>
> (Gould 2001: 450)

The law criminalising use of drugs eventually allowed for the possibility of prison sentences in 1993, four years after the criminalisation of the use of drugs came into being (UNODC 2006); this legislation also allows for stopping, searching, and compulsory blood and/or urine testing of people suspected of having used drugs (Hallam 2010). As the first below-quoted respondent argues, it is the possibility of prison which allows for such invasive interventions. Swedish drug law is thus designed to operate as a deterrent and intervention (Hallam 2010), and as a punitive measure (though the first respondent quoted below claims that incarceration solely for drug use does not occur):

> 'a person that has been caught and convicted for using drugs, that person will never go to prison. It's a technical thing, because if Swedish police... should be able to do something by force, for instance, take you into the police station, and leave a sample of urine, or a sample of blood... there has to be prison within the potential punishment'.
>
> (Interview, Stockholm Police [Narcotics Division Team Leader])

> 'It was very, very difficult for police to search people [before the law], because they have no right to do it.'
>
> (Interview, Founder of KRIS)

> '[The argument] grew and became very strong in the debate, saying that drugs are not possible to deal with in any other way but to lock people in, to increase the time that they have to spend in jail, and gradually it became more and more repressive, ending up sort of in 1988 when it became illegal to be a drug addict... To have it in your body became illegal.'
>
> (Interview, Chair of RFHL)

Compulsory care

A Commission report published in 1987 associated 'addiction' (how this is defined is arguably somewhat arbitrary, and is discussed in detail in the following chapter) with criminality, sex work, and with concerns surrounding HIV/AIDS (Gould 1989). The Commission called for improvements to voluntarily accepted care, with more training for specialised social workers. It was also argued that LVM compulsory care legislation for those deemed to be 'addicts' should be widened to include not only urgent cases, but also people who simply 'seriously worsened their living conditions'[3] (Gould 1989: 736). It was recommended that compulsory care should be increased from two to six months, with the possibility of taking an individual into immediate custody (Gould 1989; UNODC 2006). A model of 'false consciousness' was used to rationalise the compulsory treatment of people who use drugs, specifically those with drug dependency, due to their apparently diminished agency and responsibility.

False consciousness is a particular classical Marxist understanding which tells us that the agency and self-determination of certain groups (the working classes, in the context of Marxist discourse[4]) can be undermined by various sociocultural pressures and contexts, particularly subjugation, abuse, trauma, and conditioning. According to this understanding, the individual/group in question *appears* to consent to their situation/exploitation/destruction, but in actual fact cannot exercise objective reflection and reflexivity. Though this view is problematic in its patronisation and crude (and arbitrarily selective) belittlement of the autonomy and agency of marginalised and socially excluded communities, it is a potent tool in (selectively) silencing certain groups, so that others may speak in their place and establish dominant discourse. In Sweden it has not just been applied to people who use drugs, but also other groups in Swedish society, particularly sex workers, homeless people, the economically disenfranchised, and migrants. It has been used to undermine agency and self-determination through assertions that these groups lack choice and free will:

> 'it seemed to be generally accepted that most prostitution should be regarded as forced. Women were forced when they were too young to decide for themselves; as immigrants by fear of repatriation; when poor by basic material needs; and while addicts by their drug habit... Prostitutes were *forced* into the sex trade just as drug users were compelled to take drugs.'
>
> (Gould 2001: 445, 451)

Thus, where an individual does not wish to cease their drug use, this is simply attributed to the power of their 'addiction' serving to undermine their 'true' agency and consent, thus necessitating coercive and compulsory interventions: '(c) oercive practices can be justified as endeavours to assist the true self and respect its genuine desires, while wishes expressed by the individual which do not conform to the truth of addiction can be dismissed as symptoms of the disease' (Keane 2002: 191–192). The idea is that 'denial' is one particular symptom of the addiction-as-disease model (discussed further in Chapter 2) and this symptom comes to undermine the autonomy, and in turn the professed views, of people who use drugs (Keane 2002). This has come to justify – in various contexts and not only in Sweden – not only exclusion from political contribution, but also coercive and compulsory care (Keane 2002; also see Wild 2005),[5] treatment that is 'not ethical for any group, as it breaches the standard of informed consent' (Stevens 2012: 7). Dismissing the desires and informed consent (Stevens 2012) of the individual through an understanding of 'denial' as a symptom of 'addiction' (Keane 2002) is used to undermine the ability of people who use drugs to voluntarily commit themselves to rehabilitation (Anker 2007; Hallam 2010), 'an argument that originated in connection with alcohol' in Sweden (Gould 1989: 739). As noted, the 'addiction as disease' model of understanding is discussed (and critiqued) in detail in the following chapter.

> 'When you're a drug addict... it takes a long time until you say to yourself, that you want to be drug-free... It doesn't happen a lot, that a like heroin addict comes into a hospital or a treatment facility saying I want to be drug-free, it doesn't work like that. And in Sweden... you also have these laws saying that you can treat a person against his or her will'.
>
> (Interview, IOGT-NTO; Previously RNS)

> 'The first responsibility [in] my opinion is trying to help them as much as you can, and enlighten them, and in the end if they don't want to listen, try to force them to stop taking drugs, because drugs take their lives in the long term'.
>
> (Interview, Stockholm Police [Narcotics Division Team Leader])

> 'I think we should use forced treatment much more... Semi-prison like. People don't quit unless they're forced... That's always the case actually, people never quit unless they're forced to.'
>
> (Interview, RNS)

> '[It is thought that] you can't help yourself, you can't stop, and the only thing to do is lock people away. There is no other solution. Because they're out of control.'
>
> (Interview, Chair of RFHL)

People who use drugs are thus seen to require compulsory care, which is needed to free them from the pathological bonds and denial of their 'addiction' (Gould 2001). Compulsory treatment is constructed as indispensable (as per the penultimate of the above quotations), 'a logical consequence of the pursuit of the objective of a drug free society' (UNODC 2006: 15), committing to care those who cannot care for themselves (Anker 2007).

Some concern was expressed by organisations such as RFHL (discussed below) responding to the *remiss* consultation, especially voicing worries as to the extent to which compulsory care would target the most marginalised and vulnerable in society, and as to whether increasing length of treatment would yield successful results in promoting a cessation of drug use (Gould 1989; Lindberg and Haynes 2000). Additional concern was expressed as to the likelihood of this legislation driving drug use underground and disincentivising people who use drugs to seek assistance (Gould 1989).

International models: war on drugs vs drug law reform

Sweden's advocating criminalisation, forced treatment, and social-exclusion of people who use drugs from normative society has not occurred in a vacuum of policy formation internationally or, indeed, in a context of a lack of alternative and divergent discourse and understanding. Contemporarily, there may be argued to be two contrasting 'camps' of perspective, with a 'drug law reform' paradigm contrasting distinctly from a prohibitionist 'war on drugs' paradigm.[6]

Swedish prohibitionism – though radical in its actual criminalisation of the *use* of drugs – is a facet of broader 'war on drugs' rhetoric and legislative infra-structure. International 'war on drugs' approaches to drugs since the 1960s have tended to focus on attempting to reduce drug use and availability, and have involved criminalisation and control of drugs and people who use them, as well as attempts at interfering with supply and demand through policing, customs controls, and education. Politicians have frequently responded to drug-related harms not by suggesting policies that diverge from historical precedent, but by persisting with those in existence whilst calling for more prohibitive and punitive measures, as has been very much the case in Sweden (Des Jarlais 1995). To be sure, incarceration of people who use drugs – but have committed no other crime – in prisons or drug detention centres, policies which are known to contribute to the increased transmission of blood borne infections like HIV and hepatitis (as will be discussed in the following chapters), continue to receive fervent support in many quarters (Global Commission on Drug Policy 2011; Global Commission on Drug Policy 2012; Kerr and Wood 2008). People who use drugs are often uncritically and unquestioningly moralised to be 'deserving punishment rather than deserving health care' (Des Jarlais et al. 1995: 1579).

In contrast, the drug law reform camp emphasises that although numerous harms may surround illicit drug use, it is the criminalising laws and policies, along with their justificatory social constructions and stigmas, which are principally responsible for driving and worsening many of these harms. This discourse positions itself as in contradistinction to prohibition and criminalisation, in that it argues that prohibition and criminalisation are not driven by evidence of effectiveness for the reduction of harm or, for that matter, the reduction of drug use.

Where harms may be associated with drug use itself, this camp stresses that they are also intersected and exacerbated – as well as directly produced – by prohibition, criminalisation, and by the so-called 'war on drugs', all of which serve to heighten and intensify, rather than reduce or ameliorate, the damage associated with drug use (both to people who use drugs themselves, the communities in which they live, and broader society at large in addition). Moreover, it is argued that the stigma, discrimination, and social exclusion that are used to justify such laws and policies (and that are driven and exacerbated by these laws and policies in turn) serve only to compound and multiply these harms.

This camp emphasises that since prohibitionist policies have failed to decrease drug-related harms, comprehensive legal reform is necessary, with an end to the criminalisation and stigmatisation of people who use drugs 'urgently' called for (Global Commission on Drug Policy 2011). Indeed, 'decriminalisation or depenalisation of drugs for personal use have been widely recommended' (Jürgens et al. 2010), and models of decriminalisation have been adopted by various states in recent years: the use of all drugs was decriminalised by Portugal in 2001, and regulated cannabis markets in various US states and other contexts serve to highlight a shift not just towards decriminalisation of people who use drugs but towards legalised and regulated drug production also. I should stress, however, that these are considerably variable and contrasting approaches, and no state has realised a full decriminalisation of people who use drugs alongside an attendant legalisation and regulation of all drugs themselves.

A challenging alternative discourse 'based on a formal assessment of harm rather than on prejudice and assumptions' (Nutt et al. 2007: 1052; also see Tammi 2005a) is advocated as an alternative to crude and punitive criminalisation and (mis)classification. Pragmatism and nuance in terms of harm are emphasised, where 'one must move from an "all drug use is bad" stance to a "some drug use is much worse than other drug use" perspective' (Des Jarlais et al. 1995: 1579). Multicriteria analyses (Nutt et al. 2007; Nutt et al. 2010), for example, that address multiple harms – both to the individual, and to society – are inevitably more empirically grounded on evidence and realistic than policy and analysis with a foundation of assumption and unempirical generalisation.[7] In order to decrease the harms surrounding drug use, law and policy should be pragmatic and assessed empirically on real outcomes (Tammi and Hurme 2006). A move towards pragmatism, towards policies and laws based on empirical evidence of reduced harms and on a human rights and health perspective – not a punitive and moralistic one – is, in this view, the only option, where, as argued by Des Jarlais (1995: 10), 'use of psychoactive drugs is inevitable in any society that has access to such drugs. Drug policies cannot be based on a utopian belief that nonmedical drug use will be eliminated.'

Creating consensus

> 'Welcome to consensus country.'
>
> (Interview, Social Worker, Malmö Prostitution Unit; also quoted in Levy 2015)

> 'Swedes are very much a consensus, very much follow consensus generally, it's very hard for people who go outside the politically correct view… I think because we are a very homogeneous country.'
>
> (Interview, Gender Consultant; Previously *Kvinnoforum*; also quoted in Levy 2015)

Despite the above understandings of criminalisation as counterproductive, unsuccessful, and substantially detrimental, legislation criminalising the use of drugs was passed in Sweden in 1988 with broad political consensus, with the possibility of compulsory treatment for substance 'misusers' broadened in the same year also with fair consensus; there was considerable opposition from the Communist Party, but the Conservative and Centre parties and nearly all of the Social Democrats voted in favour. And this consensus is an enduring one in Sweden, where on issues concerning drugs, they continue 'to cut across traditional political loyalties' (Gould 1989: 740; also see Lindberg and Haynes 2000).

> '[There is] no NGO, no important group who are advocating that kind of idea [decriminalisation and/or legalisation of drugs]. So, in that case we are lucky, because we have a consensus in the view.'
>
> (Interview, Senior Advisor – Ministry of Social Affairs)

Below, I examine how consensus has been achieved in Sweden on such a contentious and divisive topic, and how Sweden – often, as I have stressed, perceived as a bastion of liberal democracy that prioritises the individual freedoms of its citizens – came to legislate so repressively against such a marginalised community.

The roles of RNS, FMN, and RFHL in achieving consensus

There have been specific organisations and NGOs which have played key roles in contributing to the debate, to the *remiss* consultation, and which have come to inform Sweden's 1988 legislation (Lenke and Olsson 2002). Indeed, it would be difficult to overestimate the impact some NGOs have had in the Swedish drugs debate, particularly RNS, Sweden's lobbying 'Association for a Drug-Free Society', joining with FMN (*föräldraföreningen mot narkotika*), the 'Parents' Association Against Drugs'. These two organisations vigorously lobbied the government over a considerable period, successfully campaigning for stricter and more punitive controls dealing with drug use and drug users (Gould 1989). Political influencing by RNS and FMN of Sweden's political and governmental infrastructure have been important in determining and maintaining the political contribution, interest, and substantial influence of these groups and (Gould 1989; Lindberg and Haynes 2000; UNODC 2006).

> 'From a historical point of view, I think we can say that we have been relatively successful, we've been able to influence policy by influencing political parties, decision makers in the parties, but I think mainly influencing public opinion has been more important'.
>
> (Interview, RNS)

> 'They [RNS] were very strong in the eighties. So they worked together with FMN, they became very close... they thought that the solution for their children... might be that society [should] lock them in... harder ways of doing things could correct the children. I wish they had not fell [fallen] into that trap.'
>
> (Interview, Chair of RFHL)

> '...with RNS, but there... [isn't] any balance, there aren't any organisation who really [argue] against [RNS].'
>
> (Interview, Politician – The Left Party; Former Drug User)

RNS was founded in 1969 by 'their ideological father' (Lenke and Olsson 2002: 69), the psychiatrist Nils Bejerot, known for his coining and analysis of so-called 'Stockholm Syndrome'. He and RNS were of great influence in the formation of Sweden's drug discourse in the 1970s, with the 'drug question' argued to have allowed for a political re-entry of Sweden's temperance movement, wherein lay Bejerot's ideological roots (Lenke and Olsson 2002): Bejerot 'was at the centre of the dissemination of the zero tolerance model' (Hallam 2010: 6), was consultant to the Stockholm police during the 1950s and 1960s (Hallam 2010), and had evaluated the medical prescribing practices of the mid 1960s, labelling them a catastrophe responsible for a 'Swedish drug epidemic' (Lenke and Olsson 2002: 66). Organisations alongside individual actors, then, have played no small role in influencing the drugs debate in Sweden:

> 'It was [a] huge debate in [the] seventies I would say, on, on drug policies and Nils Bejerot was one person who, I think, influenced policy, in many ways.'
> (Interview, Senior Advisor – Ministry of Social Affairs)

> 'Bejerot, you know, he's, he became kind of a public voice in Sweden'.
> (Interview, RFHL, Drug User)

As I discuss in the next chapter, for Bejerot and RNS the spread of drug use itself was and is seen to be an epidemic, with people who use drugs being the vectors of this social disease, thus threatening the wellbeing and health of the Swedish populace and the *folkhemmet* ideal. During the legal debate preceding the introduction of the criminalisation of the use of drugs, RNS advocated strong control, repression, and segregation of people who use drugs, arguing that their movement should be curtailed, with those suspected of using drugs subject to compulsory testing. FMN similarly felt that all cases of drug use should result in 'extensive investigation' and treatment (Gould 1989).

In opposition to RNS for much of the debate were RFHL; indeed, due to the considerable role of RNS and RFHL in the political debate and in framing, shaping, challenging, and reconstructing dominant and subordinate discourses, I interviewed numerous respondents from both organisations; as key respondents, their testimony is quoted throughout this book. Unlike RNS, which functions solely as a lobby organisation, RFHL, along with other organisations in the 'client movement', is composed partially of those it represents, people who use drugs, with the movement focussing upon self-determination and representation of otherwise marginalised groups. Prior to the debates of the 1980s, they had been of more significant influence, commanding credibility and power as a lobby and rights organisation:

> '[We] became quite important, because that was the first time when clients came together. Clients demanding changes... Clients saying that "we are not prepared to be objects anymore, we are supposed to be our own subjects."'
> (Interview, Chair of RFHL)

Following the high popularity and influence of RFHL, however, the organisation came to be sidelined in the context of increasing panic and concern surrounding a drug use 'epidemic', falling out of favour (or, arguably, out of popular relevance) in a discursive environment typified more and more by narratives of the need for repression, control, and social exclusion. In the instigation of prohibitionist legislation, RFHL, positioning themselves as representing the views of people who use drugs themselves, came to be perceived as somewhat obsolete, juxtaposed with the increasingly popular RNS, 'a small but vociferous group' (Gould 1989: 734):

> 'at the time we were looked upon as people with knowledge, people with experience, they were happy to learn from us. And then we had this political change when the repression grew, when the solidarity was no longer an issue.'
> (Interview, Chair of RFHL)

Absence of divergent voices

Political consensus in Sweden on the topic of drugs and drug policy has been achieved through exclusion, undermining, and belittlement of narratives that diverge from the political status quo, from dominant discourse, allowing little leeway for nuance vis-à-vis drug policy discussion, debate, and discourse. Affirming with prohibitionist 'drug-free society' discourse and being politically correct – that is, in this case, ascribing to Swedish prohibitionist dominant discourse – is essential if one wishes to be taken seriously as a commentator on drug use in Sweden and, indeed, if one wishes to continue to contribute to discussions and continue with an influential political career:

> 'In Sweden it's, political correctness is very important. There is no one today that dares say that they are not for a drug-free society. Because that would be kind of a political suicide.'
>
> (Interview, RFHL, Drug User)

> 'You can't say that there is something good with drugs. That's some kind of suicide in the, you are dead in the debate after that.'
>
> (Interview, *Svenska Brukarföreningen* Stockholm Coordinator; Former Drug User)

> 'The political agenda, it's political suicide to do anything that doesn't fit under the name "the war on drugs"'.
>
> (Interview, *Svenska Brukarföreningen*)

> 'They are not open for discussion and they maybe discuss with people, but they have already made up their minds.'
>
> (Interview, *Svenska Brukarföreningen*; Former Drug User)

Voices that do not conform to Sweden's mainstream discourse are misrepresented and caricatured. Those criticising law and discourse are conceptually (and sensationally) transmuted into 'a drug liberal who will stand by helplessly and watch young people dying and destroying their lives' (Gould 1989: 740), undermining their credibility and distancing them from debate. Though Gould's observation may seem to be dramatic, it corroborates strikingly with my observations, and that of my respondents quoted below. Indeed, the term '*drogliberal*' (drug liberal) has literally abusive connotation in Sweden (Gould 1996): simply accusing political opposition of drugs liberalism has been 'the most powerful weapon you can use' (Gould 1989: 740), with campaigning against criminalisation of drug use, or in favour of harm reduction, caricatured as being in favour of legalisation and endorsing and encouraging drug use (also see Anker 2007), diametrically opposed to Sweden's utopian and outspoken aspiration to create a drug-free society.

> 'We thought that you should take away the law who said that people is criminal if they have drugs inside [their bloodstream], and then we have to

create a situation with harm reduction. So. So now the most people from the other parties says that, I'm really liberal, I think that people should use drug everyday.'

(Interview, Politician – The Left Party; Former Drug User)

'We [RFHL] have had very, a great position in the seventies. But… at the beginning of the eighties the politics turned onto more repressive policies. And during the eighties… we were marginalised as an organisation, because they called us drug liberal, and that we were pro-drugs.'

(Interview, RFHL)

'We were [seen to be] liberals, we were drug liberals, we wanted to legalise. And we never said anything like that… the legalisation movement has been very, very small in Sweden… And that was not true, I mean we stood by our own ideas about dignity, about people's rights, etcetera.'

(Interview, Chair of RFHL)

Exclusions of drug users

It seems self-evident that it is imperative for marginalised communities themselves, such as people who use drugs and other communities like LGBTQ people and sex workers (Dodillet 2004, Levy 2015; Östergren 2004; Östergren and Dodillet 2011), to be represented in political discussion on matters that directly concern them.[8] In a context of endemic silencing of the voices of people who use drugs in political debate and discussion through an undermining of their agency and self-determination, it is hugely important for decision making, policy, research, and legislation to be informed by those to whom it pertains (see AIVL 2006; Byrne and Albers 2010; Hunt et al. 2010; Jürgens 2008). Indeed, the slogan 'nothing about us without us', first adopted by the disability rights movement, has been taken on by drug user rights organisations, both in Sweden and internationally (Jürgens 2008), emphasising the importance of their contribution and inclusion. This is reflected in client-based organisations like RFHL contributing to the aforementioned *remiss* consultation. During my fieldwork, representatives of drug user rights organisations emphasised the importance of their contribution, and the fundamental importance of them being included in debates and discussions related to policies and laws that pertain to them (INPUD 2015).

'From *Landstinget* [The County Council], it's very important for them that users should be represented just as much as possible.'

(Interview, RFHL, Drug User)

'I think that you know what's best for yourself. You know what's going to work, and you know what makes you start with drugs, and [what] was it to help you stop with drugs.'

(ibid.)

Despite the emphasised importance of the inclusion of drug users and their organisations in contributing to Swedish political discussion and debate, a model of what may be termed 'false consciousness' is used to undermine the validity and worth of the testimony of people who use drugs, 'especially those unwilling or unable to fit into the category of innocent victim' (Keane 2002: 192). This, in turn, is used to undermine the authority and legitimacy of the arguments and views of organisations comprised of people who use drugs, with the false consciousness model not only used to justify compulsory treatment for people who use drugs (as discussed above). Thus, just as people who use drugs are seen to be unable to exercise the willpower to seek rehabilitation from their problematised drug use (justifying their compulsory treatment), that same lack of agency and impotence of will – seen to be driven by people's drug dependency – is seen to justify the perception that the narratives of people who use drugs lack validity. This is linked with the discourse espoused by RNS, who argue, as per the below quotation, that people who are 'addicted' are not capable of espousing views or making decisions with a 'clear mind':

> 'I mean that once you get addicted you don't have a clear mind on these things. It's like with an alcoholic… it's no different, they're not making good choices at all, for themselves, and so this is part of the problem within the harm reduction discussion is that sort of, you listen to the addicts.'
>
> (Interview, Psychiatrist working with drug addiction; Previously with RNS)

> '[It is thought that] a drug addicted person cannot make their own assumptions. And that belongs in a very old story, Nils Bejerot.'
>
> (Interview, Social Worker, Malmö Prostitution Unit)

> 'You lose every right in the society, then the society have the right to decide everything, and because if you use drugs, [it is thought] you can't decide anything, you are damaged, and the drugs is the only thing.'
>
> (Interview, Politician – The Left Party; Former Drug User)

In Sweden, these narratives of false consciousness are not confined to engagements with drugs and people who use drugs: the Swedish paternalistic *folkhemmet* has a long history of containing and controlling marginalised communities, as has been discussed, and this has frequently been dignified and justified by undermining the agency and self-determination of the group in question, and this in turn has been informed by the ideas of feeblemindedness and eugenic inferiority that proved so popular in Sweden in the 20th century. This has notably been the case with contemporary Swedish engagements with sex work prior to and continuing on from the 1999 Swedish criminalisation of the purchase of sex.[9] It is through this systemic silencing and sidelining of sex workers and sex worker organisations in Sweden that consensus has been established on the extremely divisive topic of sex work law and policy, and a similar construction and infantilisation of people who use drugs has yielded similar results in their being silenced in and sidelined from political debate, and in the establishing of a consensus in terms of Sweden's aspiration for a 'drug-free society'.

> 'When it comes to prostitution and narcotics, that's one of the major things, I feel; that I don't know what's good for me, but my social workers does.'
>
> (Interview, RFHL, Drug User)

> 'When you have a way to look on, everything you are doing is just helping them, for their own best [good], they don't know what [is] best for themselves… you will see it even in the healthcare and social welfare system and everywhere.'
>
> (Interview, Politician – The Left Party; Former Drug User)

With the experience and agency of drug user rights activists and people who use drugs thus caricatured, undermined, and presented as unreliable, people who use drugs and their rights organisations – those whose arguments and advocated positions diverge distinctly from, and threaten to destabilise, Sweden's aspiration for a drug-free society – have historically been all but ignored in the political debate.

> 'It has always been someone that is not a drug user that has set the standard.'
>
> (Interview, *Svenska Brukarföreningen* Stockholm Coordinator; Former Drug User)

Summary: moral panic, consensus, and silencing

As was noted by one respondent, Sweden is a 'consensus country'. This is true not only in terms of drug legislation, but in terms also of legislation related to what may be considered to be divisive topics more generally in Sweden. Sweden has an established consensus on drug policy. Various key groups, notably prohibitionist groups RNS and FMN, were able to contribute significantly to the political debates that resulted in Sweden's 1988 criminalising legislation, and they advocated in support of criminalising the very use of drugs and allowing for people with drug dependencies to be forcibly treated. On the other hand, organisations reflecting the views of people who use drugs themselves, and those who advocated an evidence-based analysis involving harm reduction strategies, were increasingly silenced, undermined, and excluded.

This exclusion and silencing of some stakeholders has enabled others to establish a dominant discourse pertaining to drugs and people who use drugs: both have increasingly come to be perceived as substantial threats to the normative, rational Swedish nation state. Yet this mainstream understanding of drugs in Sweden – and legislative responses and criminalisation of substances – is far from an indicative gauge of the true harms which may be associated with drug use. Indeed, it is criminalisation itself that drives and exacerbates much of the harm associated with drug use.

Sweden's criminalisation of the use of drugs and legislation allowing for the compulsory medicalised treatment of people with drug dependency should not be seen only in the context of increasing concerns surrounding drugs themselves: racist and xenophobic moral panic surrounding the influx of foreign people and practices, coupled with concerns surrounding HIV/AIDS in the 1980s, all set the scene for radical new legislation and attendant justifying discourses. This continues Sweden's history of using legislation to address moral panics and concerns, with the law used to implement asymmetrical policies to control, contain, displace, and socially exclude those scapegoated as being responsible for threats to Swedish social order. It is these discourses and understandings of people who use drugs and of drugs themselves that I turn my attention to in the next chapter, Chapter 2, which focusses on how drugs, and the people who use them, have come to be (re)imagined and (re)constructed in Sweden. Chapter 3 will then focus on how Swedish drug legislation has been used to moralise and cleanse public space.

Notes

1 Xenophobic concern as to the ostensible risk to social order posed by migrants and people of colour – and associated practices and traditions – is by no means peculiar to Sweden. The world over, the so-called war on drugs has been shown to be a construct through which people of colour are disproportionately policed, incarcerated, subject to state-sponsored violence and, in some instances, tortured and killed (Eastwood et al. 2013; INPUD 2014).

2 Though Gould (1989) argues that Sweden's history can be seen as 'liberal' in its apparent respect for individual freedoms that do not impact broader society, this is somewhat at odds with Sweden's history of aggressively curtailing the rights of various communities. Gould's point is also made in spite of the fact that drug use in Sweden has historically been constructed not only as an issue pertaining to the individual using drugs, but also as a social and societal issue, thus not only one that should be engaged with in terms of individual freedoms 'behind closed doors' and not impacting broader society.

3 This was changed to 'runs an obvious risk of destroying his/her life' by the government (Gould 1989; UNODC 2006).

4 It should be stressed that it was Friedrich Engels who coined the term 'false consciousness', and the term does not appear in any of Marx's own writings (McCarney 2005).

5 Jürgens et al. (2010) note coercive care in Burma, Cambodia, China, Indonesia, Laos, Malaysia, Thailand, and Vietnam. Compulsory treatment also takes place in Europe, with Sweden's 'Care of Misusers' law allowing for such involuntary, coercive treatment, as is discussed in this book.

6 It must be stressed that within the 'camps' of 'prohibitionism' and 'drug law reform' exist enormous variability and divergence, and there may additionally be intersections between the two camps. For example, though decriminalisation of people who use drugs and rolling out comprehensive harm reduction interventions may be advocated by some of those in the drug law reform camp, they may not also advocate regulated and legalised production and distribution of currently illegal and/or controlled psychoactive drugs.

7 This language of which drugs are '*worse*' than others may be argued not to progress discourse and debate radically enough, since it may be argued that we must move away from conflations of all drug use as detrimental and problematic, and acknowledge the plethora of motives and experiences of people in using various drugs in various ways, a concession that some drug use is much *safer* than other drug use and that drug use can be *beneficial* and *pleasurable*. It is, in fact, argued by drug user rights organisations

(amongst others) that to use drugs is a human right, and that interfering with people's drug use through criminalisation, stigmatisation, and discrimination violates human rights to privacy, to bodily integrity, and to the highest attainable standard of health, to name but a few (INPUD 2015).

8 The need for the meaningful involvement of marginalised communities in discussions that relate to them is not the only parallel in these groups' experience of difficulties, where those faced by marginalised, stigmatised, and/or criminalised communities – including people who use drugs, sex workers, LGBTQ communities – are similar. It is no coincidence that this same 'nothing about us without us' slogan has been taken on by sex worker activists, where sex workers can face the same opposition to the implementation of sex work-related harm reduction initiatives, and similar issues relating to marginalisation, disempowerment, and an undermining of agency, a group whose own contribution to the formation of law and policy is also advocated in the context of their absence and exclusion (see International Sex Worker Harm Reduction Caucus 2008; Rekart 2005; UNAIDS 2009). A need to recognise and maximise opportunities and efforts of marginalised communities to organise, network, and peer-educate has been argued to be key as a means to the end of exclusion and the promotion of rights and health (AIVL 2006; Brooks-Gordon 2006; Hunt et al. 2010; Jürgens 2008; Sanders and Campbell 2007; Scambler et al. 1990; UNAIDS 2009; Ward 2007).

9 Sex workers are, in Sweden, generalised, infantilised, and pathologised as traumatised victims of patriarchal violence and childhood abuse, and they are thus discursively rendered as unable to make objective and informed decisions about themselves, their lives, and their communities and families, and the validity of their narratives and testimony is undermined in turn (for authors who espouse these arguments see Farley 2006; Jeffreys 1997; for analysis of this in the case of Swedish sex work see Levy 2015). Such constructions have resulted in the silencing of sex workers in the Swedish debate (what I term 'modes of silencing' [Levy 2015]), and in organisations and stakeholders positioning themselves as experts in place of sex workers themselves, asserting a mandate to speak on sex workers' behalves following on from the narratives of sex workers being purported to be misleading and inaccurate (Levy 2015; *Socialstyrelsen* [National Board of Health and Welfare] 2008).

2 Reimagining drugs (and people who use them)

What may be perceived to be radical and/or drastic legislation, such as Sweden's criminalisation of the use of drugs and Sweden's legislation allowing for compulsory treatment of people with drug and alcohol dependency, is often accompanied by social construction and understanding: a problem must be established to be legislated against, and circularly, the legislation then constructs and essentially identifies the problem, whilst identifying what is a normatively acceptable ideal. Discourses of normativity and normative acceptability on the one hand, and discourses of deviance on the other, are thus circularly produced. And this is particularly the case then in Sweden, where Sweden is something of an extreme example when it comes to (re)defining and (re)imagining what are constructed to be social problems, and establishing consensus and disseminating dominant discourse (*how* dominant discourse is disseminated in Sweden will be of greater focus in Chapter 5 particularly).

In this chapter, I discuss how drugs, and people who use drugs, have come to be understood in Sweden.[1] I begin by discussing how Swedish prohibitionist legislation has served as a means with which to send signals to broader Swedish society as to what is expected of citizens of the Swedish People's Home. I then move onto discussions of specific social constructions, first of people who use drugs, and then of how drugs themselves have come to be imagined and normalised in some cases, and constructed as deviant and problematic in others. Much of the discussion of this chapter is grounded in terms of broader discourses surrounding drug use and people who use drugs, as well as discourses surrounding the construction of what is often referred to as the 'addiction-as-disease' model, though, as will become clear, the intricacies of Swedish understandings of drugs and drug users are peculiar to Sweden. Disease and pathologisation are recurrent themes in this chapter, as is an attendant demonisation and infantilisation of people who use drugs, all of which has informed Sweden's repressive, prohibitionist drugs legislation.

Sending a signal and political posturing

> 'By making drug-use a criminal offence, society would be making it clear that it was an unacceptable activity. This would have an important psychological and symbolic effect.'
>
> (Gould 1989: 733)

> 'It is a Swedish mentality, it's difficult to describe it, but it is a Swedish mentality of society knowing best, making people objects. This is the way we do things in Sweden you know.'
>
> (Interview, Chair of RFHL; also quoted in Levy 2015)

Criminalising the use of drugs is and was intended to act as a deterrent, to send a signal that drug use is not acceptable in Swedish society, and compulsory treatment should moreover be seen as part of this message (UNODC 2006; Van der Giessen and Van Brussel 1996): using drugs will result in state interventions, and punitive and compulsory repercussions. Actually decreasing drug use and achieving a drugs-free society may therefore be regarded as peripheral to Sweden's political posturing and positioning itself as a state that does not tolerate drugs and drug use; that it unrealistically aims to eliminate drug use entirely (as per the penultimate quotation below), is sidelined in preference to a focus on sending this societal signal, with Swedish drugs legislation acting as a medium through which dominant discourse has been established and disseminated throughout the people of the Swedish *folkhemmet* (and to those internationally observing Sweden's stance on drugs). And public opinion supporting Swedish drugs policy has remained strong (also see EMCDDA 2008), a testament to Sweden's successes in creating consensuses and establishing dominant discourse:

> 'It's about signals… that's what it's all about. That's the main pillar… That's why, "Is the political ideas and signals more important than saving lives?" is a question we always ask politicians.'
>
> (Interview, Chair and Founder of *Svenska Brukarföreningen*; Drug User)

> '…majority, or no public opinion in favour of using illicit drugs. We tried to keep that as hard as possible, 'cause that's the best prevention technique… If everyone think that you shouldn't, we shouldn't use illicit drugs, which is, in one way a drug-free society, a society where drugs are not a normal part of a life.'
>
> (Interview, Senior Advisor – Ministry of Social Affairs)

> 'The ultimate objective is a drug-free society. We are sometimes criticised for that, because it's not, some people think it's not realistic. And then we say, "why should we have realistic objectives? This is our intention. Our direction… this is the ultimate goal."'
>
> (ibid.)

> 'We can't close our borders, we can't stop the use of the internet, we can't, I mean the drugs will always be there.'
>
> (Interview, Stockholm Police [Narcotics Division Team Leader])

Moral posturing amongst political parties and politicians, who attempted to outdo one another in expressions of prohibitionist sentiment, can be seen to have impacted the political debate and fed into the aforementioned prohibitionist political consensus. No doubt this was also linked to the fact that coming out as being opposed to the prevailing prohibitionist discourse in Sweden can be political suicide, as one respondent stressed in the previous chapter.

> 'It has been an easy way of getting high profile as a politician.'
>
> (Interview, RFHL)

> 'The political parties on election times for instance, they had some kind of a race, who showed more muscles... Who is the most repressive? 'Oh, we will really deal with this. Give us the power and we will deal with this'. And they all agreed on it sort of.'
>
> (Interview, Chair of RFHL)

And the messages that have been sent to the society of the *folkhemmet* – both related to the unacceptability of drugs, and to the people who use them – have been politically appealing, as discussed in the previous chapter: whilst organisations such as RFHL and *Svenska Brukarföreningen*, who attempt to introduce complexity and nuance, and who attempt to challenge and complicate generalisations, have been historically sidelined in political debate and discussion, other organisations, like the prohibitionist RNS, have been politically attractive and have become instrumental in informing policy.

> 'RNS, I mean, I have no hope. No hope at all. They are losing power, they are losing members, they are fewer. But still there is a political interest in organisations like that, because organisations like that feed in very well to the political ideas.'
>
> (Interview, Chair of RFHL)

> 'At the end of the day you have a [purported] solution, of course that is what we all are dreaming about. And RFHL is always explaining things in a quite complicated way.'
>
> (ibid.)

Drug use as disease, drug users as vectors

The fundamental problematisation of drug use and people who use drugs in Sweden is rooted in what may be termed the 'addiction-as-disease' model, in a pathologisation of people who use drugs, with drug dependence coming to be understood and constructed as a disease displaying a specific (though variable and changeable) set of symptoms (see Jellinek 1960; also see Keane 2002; Larkin et al. 2006; Vrecko 2010). I do not wish to spend considerable time debating the merits of addiction-as-disease here. But it is important to emphasise that this perception is both problematic and contentious. The basis of the construction of addiction-as-disease is little more than it deviates from a condition seen to be normative (Room 2005), a condition which is variable and reconstructed in differing contexts and times; addiction thus seems wholly different from empirically and consistently demonstrable 'disease'. As Keane emphasises in her involved deconstruction and exploration of the history of narratives and discourses of addiction,

> '[t]he more effort is put into finding answers, the more questions keep proliferating. What kind of thing is addiction? Is it a disease or a syndrome or a psychological process? Is it a metaphorical disease or a real one (and what exactly is the difference)? If it is a disease what are its symptoms? How do its physical, psychological and social factors interact and what is their relative importance?'
>
> (Keane 2002: 10)

Apparent symptoms and signifiers of addiction-as-disease are uncertain, contextual, and mutable, hardly symptoms of a demonstrable disease, more signifiers of a *discourse* of addiction, in that it has come to be asserted that the disease of addiction is natural, immutable, unchangeable, and 'true'; but in fact addiction-as-disease is socially produced and constructed. As argued by Reinarman,

> '[a]ddiction-as-disease is not as discrete or as readily identifiable an entity as many people believe it is. One of the principal reasons for this is that the user behaviors presumed to constitute it are protean, forged in interaction with features of users' environments. What are taken as empirical indicators of an underlying disease of addiction consist of a broad range of behaviors that are interpreted as "symptoms" only under some circumstances. They can be aggregated to fit under the heading of "addiction" only by means of some degree of epistemic force.'
>
> (Reinarman 2005: 307)

The meaning and (questionable) ontology of 'addiction' is therefore not clear, consistent, or stable. The World Health Organization recommended as early as the 1960s that the terms 'addiction' and 'addict' be abandoned in favour of 'dependence', arguably a more nuanced, less reductive *descriptor* as opposed to the muddy identity/disease label of 'addict/addiction', yet, the terms addict/addiction are still commonly used by healthcare professionals, in mainstream parlance (WHO n.d.), and in Swedish dominant discourse and political and medical discussion.

In Sweden, this discourse was reimagined and constructed famously (or notoriously) by RNS founder Nils Bejerot, 'sometimes referred to as the founding father of Swedish drug control policy' (UNODC 2006: 12). This 'very strange doctor' (Interview, Chair of RFHL) conceived the *spread* of drugs as itself a transmissible, contagious epidemic disease (Lenke and Olsson 2002; Lindberg and Haynes 2000). Although the construction of *addiction* as disease with a discrete set of symptoms is by no means a new concept, the construction of all drug *use* and its spread as disease and epidemic, irrespective of dependence or 'addiction', is something peculiar to Swedish constructions of drug use, driven by Bejerot's ideas and theories. It should be stressed that this conceptualisation does not engage with the possible societal harms that may be associated with drug dependency, drug use, and/or criminalisation, such as theft to acquire substances and so forth: drug use is, in and of itself, characterised as a socially detrimental, contagious disease. The Swedish metaphor of drug use as a disease in-and-of-itself, was recurrent during my interviews and fieldwork, with people who use drugs understood as 'infecting' other individuals through providing them with drugs and/or teaching them how to use and acquire substances, and this was described as 'an 'epidemic addiction'' spread 'usually after direct personal initiation from another drug abuser' (UNODC 2006: 12), with drug use argued in Sweden to be as powerful as natural instincts and primitive urges (Bejerot 1972; also see Hallam 2010). With their apparent capability of precipitating the spread of drugs through the Swedish populace, people who use drugs are thus constructed as an urgent threat to normative Swedish society, threatening the wellbeing of the entire population and of the Swedish *folkhemmet* nation state at large (Gould 1996).

> 'If you have this one person, that shows the other nine, then you have ten people carrying this disease, ten people that has acquired the knowledge how to smoke [drugs], and they could be experienced carriers for a lot of new young kids.'
>
> (Interview, Stockholm Police [Narcotics Division Team Leader])

> '[It is felt that] I infect people with my disease. Or I am the disease, and I should therefore be isolated from society.'
>
> (Interview, RFHL, Drug User)

> 'He [Bejerot] talked a lot about this academic view, like, that a drug user… transmit to somebody with their disease. And so maybe he said it in that kind of term… isolate those people so that they cannot spread it, maybe.'
>
> (Interview, IOGT-NTO; Previously RNS)

Legislation allowing for isolation and compulsory treatment of people who use drugs, as well as policies that result in a containment and displacement of people who use drugs (discussed in the following chapters) should thus be seen to result, in part, from what is believed to be the societal risk which people who use drugs pose in terms of their potential to transmit their 'disease' of drug use to others. In the past, RNS have radically suggested an isolation of some people who use drugs to islands in the Swedish archipelago, essentially forming isolated camps, concentrating the populations of people who use drugs to secure, excluded, and contained areas, a situation of literal social exclusion reminiscent of the lock hospitals of the 19th century, in which people with various contagious and/or venereal diseases were forcibly confined and treated. This advocated action of isolation has two drivers: firstly, the protection of society from the ostensible threat of 'infection' of the 'epidemic disease' of drug use. Secondly, the imposition of treatment (which has been realised through other means) on people who are constructed – through the pathologisation and infantilisation of the addiction-as-disease model – as being mentally incapable of making decisions for their own good. This again must be seen in the context of Sweden's history of eugenics and violent social engineering; the legislation allowing for the compulsory treatment of people with drug dependencies does not, perhaps, seem so drastic or incongruous with the backdrop of these other draconian and repressive interventions that were, in fact, advocated by those very same stakeholders who shaped Sweden's drug law, policy, and discourse preceding 1988.

> 'He [Nils Bejerot] said there are certain groups of addicts… [who] do not have a criminal lifestyle at all… I could accept that there would be a need for having closed villages, why not, on an island, where they would live and we could give them drugs, but the important thing is that they don't spread it to others. That's sort of harm reduction… those who would be affected by it would like it very much, most likely. I mean, if you take a heroin addict and say "You can live in this flat, we're going to come to you with heroin every day". "Wonderful, paradise."'
>
> (Interview, RNS)

> 'In the sixties, one doctor turned up named Nils Bejerot. And he saw drug users as a virus… He's a really dangerous man, but he's dead now… So he, actually he named a few islands up north Sweden, where he said "We put all the drug users there, we give them the drugs and they can kill themselves, because they are a virus."'
>
> (Interview, Chair and Founder of *Svenska Brukarföreningen*; Drug User)

Drug users: pathologisation and infantilisation

With drug use and drug dependence constructed as disease, people who use drugs are themselves heavily pathologised as these diseases' carriers and wanton transmitters. Though the stigma that can surround psychoactive drugs is variable, with the moderate and contextual use of drugs such as alcohol not necessarily seen in a negative light, the stigma surrounding 'addiction' and 'addicts' is 'generalised and ubiquitous' (Room 2005). People who use drugs and people seen to be 'addicts' are *assumed* to be lying, manipulative, problematic (Ning 2005), and dirty (Room 2005); we can see how these assumptions tie in with loaded terms such as 'clean', discussed in this book's Introduction. Simply, the term 'addict' is so imbued with these negative connotations that they need little by way of specific mention. The double-edged stigma of pathology and criminality, or, put another way, of disease and (im)morality (Larkin et al. 2006) that surrounds people who use drugs in many societies informs 'the traditional view in which the user is perceived as either a criminal or a sick person' (Tammi and Hurme 2006: 2).

In Sweden, therefore, a reductive totalisation follows. People are seen through a lens of their drug use, with perception being that 'everything you do connects to the fact that you use drugs… It's the only thing about you that exists really. You are like reduced to some drug using organism' (Interview, *Svenska Brukarföreningen* Stockholm Coordinator; Former Drug User). This ties in with constructions of addictive personalities, something (genetic or circumstantial) that predestines a 'certain type of person' to use substances or to become 'addicted' (Larkin et al. 2006). A respondent from Stockholm Police's Narcotics Division drew a comparison between drug use and sex work, feeling that drug consumption or sex selling were undertaken as efforts to fill some sort of psychological flaw or void:

> 'there is always something in the background, and I think it's [the] exact same thing with drugs and drug users. People have something that they are missing in their life, and they fill that hole with drugs, and I think also that [is the case for] women that are prostitutes.'
>
> (Interview, Stockholm Police [Narcotics Division Team Leader])

Such generalisations of drug use result in very little differentiation being made between different people who use drugs, or, as is discussed in greater detail below, between the drugs themselves which people use.

> '[There is a] lack of nuance… Everything is just black or white. They miss all the shades of grey.'
>
> (Interview, *Svenska Brukarföreningen* Stockholm Coordinator; Former Drug User)

> '…make you into a certain kind of person, it makes you into a stupid junkie'.
>
> (ibid.)

> '…attitudes, and the criminalisation who [that] started up all these attitudes. It's illegal to do drugs, it's not a health issue, it's a question of law.'
>
> (Interview, Chair and Founder of *Svenska Brukarföreningen*; Drug User)

> 'I still know a lot of people who just use drugs sometimes, and sometimes for weekends, sometimes for not taking anything for a long time… they are still living a, quite social life, and have work and families… that's a side that the most politicians, they don't believe that that exists… But you don't see them, because you don't see them hanging around *Plattan* [a large square in the centre of the Stockholm well known as an area where drugs are bought and sold].'
>
> (Interview, Politician – The Left Party; Former Drug User)

People who use drugs are universally demonised, characterised as malicious, dangerous, and untrustworthy; 'if you are a drug user in Sweden, (it is thought that) you can't be trusted. You always got a hidden agenda' (Interview, *Svenska Brukarföreningen* Stockholm Coordinator; Former Drug User), tying in with 'conventional paradigms' constructing 'addicts as liars, fabricators, and manipulators' (Ning 2005: 349). This characterisation ties in with how the views and experiences of people who use drugs have been discounted and excluded in political discussion and debate, made not to count through their being undermined as (at best) disingenuous and misleading, and also tying in with how Sweden justifies state-sponsored intervention and treatment. As discussed, during 1980s legal debates and in the media, drug use has also come to be automatically associated with apparent social and moral ills such as sex work, criminality, and the spread of HIV (Lenke and Olsson 2002).

In addition to being constructed as mendacious, pathological, and dangerous criminals, those with drug dependencies are paradoxically seen through the addiction-as-disease model as being rendered helpless by 'addiction', serving to undermine agency and self-determination: the addiction-as-disease model sees individuals 'infantilised and pathologised by the presumption of powerlessness' (Keane 2002: 191), and this is very much the case in prevailing Swedish understandings. This discourse has moreover facilitated a marginalisation and silencing of the voices of people who use drugs themselves, especially those who do not wish to identify conformingly as passive, pathological 'victims' (Keane 2002), thus again serving to exclude narratives of people who use drugs from political debate and discourse. This process of undermining contribution and testimony may be seen to be a self-serving and self-supporting one, silencing those voices and contributions that may threaten to destabilise and muddy these very same crude assumptions and understandings of drug users as mentally unstable and lacking agency and/or as dangerous criminals.

And so, in Sweden, alongside an idea of deviance and danger is one of infantilisation, an undermining of the autonomy and self-determination of people who use drugs, and this feeds through to a perceived need for people who use drugs to be disciplined, educated, excluded, and sometimes subjected to compulsory treatment for their own good:

> 'there are lots of people who feel sorry for people with drug problems. Lots of people do. The other half, or something like that, who despise people with drug problems.'
>
> (Interview, RFHL)

> 'When you get addicted, you sort of develop a second personality, that is sort of living side-by-side with your own self.'
>
> (Interview, Psychiatrist working with drug addiction; Previously with RNS)

> 'In the beginning… they [drug addicts] are going to try to manipulate you'.
>
> (ibid.)

> 'I just think that people are better people if they try and succeed to stay sober and drug-free. They're better people.'
>
> (Interview, RNS)

> 'We [are thought of to] always tend to lie, to cheat, to steal, we're dangerous... you're kind of stigmatised and you're demonised as if you're very dangerous and at the same time you're marginalised because you're obviously not knowing what's best for yourself – A bit, you know, childish and stupid, at the same time that you're dangerous.'
>
> (Interview, RFHL, Drug User)

> 'I can't think [of] a group that are, have a more difficult life, and that they're more hated and less liked than [a] drug user.'
>
> (Interview, *Svenska Brukarföreningen* Stockholm Coordinator; Former Drug User)

So, where – as per a quotation above – some people 'feel sorry for' people who use drugs and others 'despise' them, these two understandings are far from mutually exclusive, going hand-in-hand as two sides of the same disempowering and generalising coin, with people who use drugs sometimes simultaneously seen to be dangerous and manipulative (despicable), as well as infantile, sick, and lacking in self-determination (pitiable). As was the case with the discussions of false consciousness in the previous chapter, these constructions of people who use drugs feed into a process of political silencing. Testimony or activism can be readily sidelined where it is assumed that

> 'if I say something, it's something that I say because I'm manipulative or I'm just lying.'
>
> (Interview, RFHL, Drug User)

Are all drugs bad?

Swedish conflations

In Sweden, distinctions between drugs, defined for example according to relative harm along the lines of 'hard' and 'soft' drug categories, are understood as fallacious (Gould 1996; Van der Giessen and Van Brussel 1996). *All* drug consumption is perceived to be dangerous and potentially 'addictive', and *all* drug use is spoken of as *missbruk*, an 'abuse' or 'misuse' (with the Swedish Drug Users' Union, *Svenska Brukarforeningen*, being a notable exception in its use of 'brukar', or 'user', as opposed to 'misuser'). Indeed, distinction is not made between 'problematic' and non-problematic use (irrespective of how this is defined[2]), and little differentiation is made between those with dependencies, and those who may be classed people who use drugs 'recreationally' or infrequently, thus blurring boundaries and simplifying intricate and variable drugs, consumption patterns, and individuals' engagements with their own drug use.

> 'When you talk about illicit drugs... any nonmedical use of that drug would be an abuse or a misuse, there is no sort of "use" of that drug... We don't talk about "recreational", "experimental", "problematic."'
>
> (Interview, RNS)

> 'In the Swedish debate, if you are using drugs, there is no difference if you are like smoking pot at the weekends, or you are injecting heroin every day. Like, in the debate, you are a drug user, and drug users are just the same.'
>
> (Interview, *Svenska Brukarföreningen* Stockholm Coordinator; Former Drug User)

A Police Narcotics Division Team Leader (Interview, 2009) indeed felt that all illicit drugs were detrimental, and that attempts at distinguishing between substances and different patterns of drug use were simply a reflection that '(t)here are degrees in hell'. Indeed, he noted that a crude drugs 'horror propaganda' had occurred in the late 1970s and the early 1980s, espousing the notion that 'if you smoke a joint, you will end up with a heroin injection in your arm'.

These crude Swedish conflations of all drugs as 'bad' heavily diverge from empirical, evidence-based approaches which are based on an understanding that there are nuanced, variable, and divergent effects – and harms – that can result from the use of various drugs in various ways, approaches that emphasise a need to engage with some drugs as being considerably more harmful than others, both to society and the individual. Indeed, the Swedish model of criminalisation, as with other prohibitionist models, may be argued to be driven by 'fundamental scientific errors', by bad pharmacology, bad sociology, bad economics (Des Jarlais 1995), and by a 'politicization and misrepresentation of science' (Kerr and Wood 2008: 964). Understandings of drug-related harm and effect within the context of a criminalising paradigm, as in Sweden (and the vast majority of other states besides!), may be argued not to be reflective of empirical true risk or cost. Criminalising legislation and discourses that construct and generalise drugs as 'bad' therefore do not reflect the variable harms that may result from the use of various drugs (Nutt et al. 2007; Nutt 2009; Nutt et al. 2010), instead confusing and convolutedly conflating attitudes and assumptions regarding the moral (un)acceptability of drugs, of people who use drugs, of psychoactive adulteration, and of resultant harms to wider society and to individuals.

Drug criminalisation classification systems and conflations of controlled and criminalised drugs should thus be regarded as entirely misleading in their purporting to be indicative benchmarks of evidence-based harm. Processes by which harms are ostensibly demonstrated – through drugs being criminalised and scheduled due supposedly to their harm – are arguably capricious, arbitrary, generalising, and moralistic (Degenhardt and Hall 2012). A 'multicriteria' decision analysis for classifying drugs has been, in contrast, proposed (Nutt et al. 2007; Nutt et al. 2010; also see Taylor et al. 2012 for a similar analysis), and this uses numerous harm criteria that are identified and weighted to address their varying gravities, with some harms and/or costs pertaining to the individual using drugs, and others to wider society. Perhaps unsurprisingly, the findings of these studies do not correlate with legal drug classifications, such as those in the UK (the focus of the studies) (Nutt et al. 2010: 1558). In fact, such studies highlight that *alcohol* is the most harmful psychoactive substance used (Nutt et al. 2010) – quite ironic given its legality (and considerable popularity, as I discuss elsewhere in this book) in states like Sweden.

Conflations of all drugs as 'bad' additionally distracts from the fact that it is criminalisation of drugs *per se* that serves to drive many of the harms that are associated with drug use (as is discussed in the following chapters), particularly in making drugs themselves so dangerous. As stressed by Stevens (2012: 9), 'critics would argue that prohibition itself is responsible for a substantial proportion of drug-related harm'. Prohibition results in drugs being produced in a black market context, which in turn results in people who use (and sell) drugs having little idea as to the composition, purity, or potential contamination of said substances. In short, prohibition and criminalisation creates a system whereby the drugs people use are of dangerously unpredictable composition, and so prohibition essentially justifies itself by *creating* more dangerous drugs. Therefore, a 'distinctive characteristic of drug policy is the prominence and variety of unintended consequences, primarily negative' (Reuter and Trautmann 2007: 46). Two recent, illustrative examples bear noting: firstly, although ecstasy/MDMA is considerably safer to the individual than many other substances, including alcohol (Nutt et al. 2007; Nutt et al. 2010), production on an unregulated, illegal black market has resulted in numerous deaths due to contamination with PMA (*para*-Methoxyamphetamine) (Levy et al. 2013; Pidd 2013); PMA is a highly dangerous compound, resulting in high morbidity and mortality (Caldicott et al. 2003). Secondly, several people have contracted anthrax from contaminated heroin in recent years (Press Association 2012). In both cases, the harms described above stem from their criminalisation and black market production and provision, rather than from the drugs themselves. That drugs result in harm and deaths as a result of contamination with toxins, or as a result of unpredictable purity, is not indicative of the harms of drug use, but instead of the unsafe and illicit production of drugs and the fact that individuals are unable to guarantee or establish the quality or nature of the drugs they buy. Criminalisation and prohibition, therefore, ironically, circularly, and perversely justify themselves by serving to create and/or exacerbate harms, a vicious cycle that further amplifies harm to both the consumers of the drugs, and to wider society. It is something of an irony then, that Sweden conflates all drugs as equally dangerous and harmful, and the legislation such conflations justify is responsible for making the drugs more dangerous.

Some drugs better than others: Swedish national drugs

Alcohol

In spite of aspiring to create a drug-free society, alcohol remains legal, commercially available, and popular in Sweden despite evidence that alcohol is significantly more individually and socially harmful than many illicit substances (Nutt et al. 2007; Nutt et al. 2010).

> '[D]rinking alcohol is very accepted in Sweden. And I think especially when it comes to young people, that is a very like, how you say, strong signal, that this is okay, if even adults drink publicly.'
>
> (Interview, IOGT-NTO; Previously RNS)

'...we're drinking so heavily in Sweden.'

(Interview, RFHL)

Alcohol and an 'intoxication oriented drinking pattern' (Boekhout van Solinge 1997: 64) have historical and cultural significance in Sweden (Gould 1996; Hallam 2010), with non-alcoholic drugs perceived as presenting more contemporary and foreign problems and threats without the same traditional Swedish roots and cultural justifications (Interview, Chair of RFHL). Alcohol is seen to allow Swedish people a release from social expectations and constraints (Boekhout van Solinge 1997), and is furthermore associated with ideas of Swedish (hetero)masculinity, with Swedish men traditionally manufacturing their own alcohol.

> 'We have a tradition of doing [making] your own alcohol... it's cultural, and traditional, it's like, you know, you should be your own man, you should hunt your own meat in the woods, and you should... do your own alcohol.'
>
> (Interview, Stockholm Police [Narcotics Division Team Leader])

Indeed, alcohol consumption is so normalised that even a representative of RNS I interviewed – a staunchly and vociferously anti-drug organisation – discussed his alcohol drinking, in spite of his and his organisation's vehemently, aggressively, and successfully campaigning for a 'drug-free society'.

> 'If alcohol had been the new [drug], it would have been totally banned, because alcohol is also [a] big source to problems... people doing crazy, crazy things on alcohol, so it's a drug like all other drugs, but I think that the difference... between, for instance, alcohol and cannabis, is that alcohol... has been in the picture for, I don't know, since the first Swede put his foot on this land.'
>
> (Interview, Stockholm Police [Narcotics Division Team Leader])

> 'There is a main support for the idea that people should be able to drink. We have the opposite situation [than is the case for illicit drugs].'
>
> (Interview, Senior Advisor – Ministry of Social Affairs)

> 'We have an alcohol culture for thousands of years... it's no meaning in having a law that is not attainable.'
>
> (Interview, Psychiatrist working with drug addiction; Previously with RNS)

The final quotation above, noting the impossibility of abolishing alcohol consumption, can be contrasted with the same respondent's advocating efforts and laws to achieve a drug-free society, with the respondent justifying both in terms of cultural tradition. Ignoring a scientific consensus that alcohol is significantly more individually and socially harmful than many illicit substances, this respondent emphasised that 'the reason why these substances are illegal is they are more dangerous' than alcohol. Indeed, were legal classification systems actually informed by empirically calculated relative harm, alcohol and tobacco, which are extensively used (and enjoyed) in Sweden, would have harm classifications in line with some of the most stigmatised and criminalised drugs on the market (Nutt et al. 2007: 1052). It is indeed sobering to note that the only reason this respondent appears to feel that alcohol should have legal status in Sweden is its cultural standing, its traditional *Swedish* use, its being intrinsic to the Swedish way of life, with the unattainability of a goal of an *alcohol*-free Swedish society justifying a dismissal of such an aim, in contrast to Sweden's aim of a *drug*-free society, hailed in paradox as ambitious and praiseworthy.

Alcohol is still understood in Sweden to be dangerous and in need of heavy regulation. It was only in 1955 that alcohol ration books were abolished (Gould 1989), and alcohol and alcoholism have been regarded as moral issues throughout much of the 20th century (Lenke and Olsson 2002). Indeed, there was awareness amongst respondents that 'if alcohol would be introduced today… then it wouldn't be legal, right?' (Interview, IOGT-NTO; Previously RNS). However, because it is seen to be an indispensable facet of the traditional *folkhemmet*, the drug of alcohol is granted exemption from Sweden's utopian vision of a drug-free society.

Swedes are paternalistically seen to be unable to moderate their own drinking, in need of strict state control and intervention (Van der Giessen and Van Brussel 1996); my quotation of Henriksson and Ytterberg (1992: 335) in this book's introduction bears repeating, with their casting the Swedish state as 'acting as a Good Parent… driven to look after its children, to assure that they behaved, that they didn't drink too much'. Current policy is of a heavily restrictive, state-interventionist approach (Tammi 2005b). System Bolaget is a state monopoly on alcohol sales; outside of this *Systemet*, only light 3.5% alcohol-by-volume beer (*folköl* or 'people's beer') may be sold by shops. Spirits are sold only by System Bolaget at hugely inflated prices and the minimum age to purchase alcohol is 20, though one may drink alcohol in licensed bars and pubs from 18. In order to discourage social drinking, refrigerated alcohol cannot be purchased from System Bolaget, and only individual items can be bought (though numerous individual items can be bought at the same time), not numerous items gathered together in a packaged pack (for example, a six-pack of beer would be out of the question). Without these strict alcohol controls, violence and vandalism are felt to be in danger of escalation; and a masculinisation of alcohol consumption and production has followed through into concerns surrounding men's violence against women and domestic violence, which is seen in Sweden as something of an historical embarrassment in need of aggressive legal and policy intervention (Elman 2001; Gould 2001; Harrington 2012; Levy 2015). Strict controls on alcohol sales are seen to reduce the incidence of these alcohol-fuelled forms of violence:

> 'that's why we have the monopoly, you know, because if we wouldn't, then the problem would be [worse]… I mean, imagine, we have these problems, if we wouldn't have System Bolaget, then we would have so much more

> problem with, with alcohol, and connection to violence is very, very strong, and, you know the beating of wives.'
>
> (Interview, IOGT-NTO; Previously RNS)

> 'Official policy is to reduce the total consumption as a way of reducing the problems connected with... alcohol.'
>
> (Interview, Senior Advisor – Ministry of Social Affairs)

System Bolaget is furthermore perceived and marketed as allowing for a greater choice of products than is available in other nations (indeed, as having 'everything', per the below quotation); this is entirely untrue, with most large supermarkets in the UK, France, and Italy (the list goes on) offering a better selection of wines, beers, and spirits, not to mention shops that specialise in, for example, whiskeys or wines, which would be illegal in Sweden. Television advertisements whilst I lived in Sweden emphasised that System Bolaget's prices needed to be elevated to such an extent in order to allow Swedes such wide selection in their alcoholic purchases. Again, we see Sweden to be trying to create an (illusory) image of itself intra- and internationally as being ahead of other states and cultures, with a more responsible and *rational* system of alcohol provision that additionally claims to be superior and more sophisticated.

> 'If you go into liquor store in Denmark, you can't find one tenth of the different type of wines that you can find at System Bolaget. System Bolaget has everything.'
>
> (Interview, Stockholm Police [Narcotics Division Team Leader]).

Snus

Similarly to alcohol, nicotine use is not seen to conflict with the ambition to realise a drug-free Sweden, and tobacco is commonly and legally available. Snus – a form of Swedish oral tobacco placed between the lip and the teeth with the nicotine absorbed through the mucus membranes of the mouth – is used by many Swedish people (Furberg et al. 2005), with around 26% of adult male and 6% of female Swedes using the substance (svensktsnus.se accessed 30/05/12). Like alcohol, snus is seen to be traditional, and like alcohol is tied in with ideas of hetero-normative Swedish machismo and masculinity (also see Gould 1996) and also with (masculinised) national identity:

> 'if you take snus away from [a] Swedish man, that's like taking a penis from a man I think.'
>
> (Interview, Stockholm Prostitution Unit)

Snus is advocated as a form of legitimate harm reduction for smokers (see Furberg et al. 2005; Gartner et al. 2007; Zhu et al. 2009), in stark contrast to harm reduction being an extremely contentious issue when applied to drug use, discussed in Chapter 4 and 5.

> 'This *holding snus* is harm reduction for cigarette smokers, you could say. *respondent inserts snus between teeth and lips* This drug is harm reduction for cigarette smokers. But every little piece that you put under your lip, contains, I think they say it contains about ten times as much nicotine as a cigarette. So the amount of nicotine in this drug is very strong... they constantly debate this in Sweden, if it's bad for your health or not.'
>
> (Interview, Stockholm Police [Narcotics Division Team Leader])

The above-quoted respondent spitting out his snus and inserting a fresh sachet during interview is somewhat ironic, given his position of enforcing Sweden's ambition to become a drug-free state! Gould (1996) indeed aesthetically compares – from the perspective of those not familiar with the practice(s) – the oral use of snus with the injecting of heroin. Despite snus' construction as normative and traditional, I have witnessed first-time users of snus – who had not built up a nicotine tolerance – suffer from an overwhelming nicotine rush, and have – on several occasions – observed the high levels of nicotine in snus induce vomiting. Snus remains illegal for commercial sale throughout the EU, though such is the perceived importance of snus as a national Swedish drug that Sweden attained exemption before becoming an EU member state (Gould 1996). All this is in stark juxtaposition to discussions and banning of khat in Sweden, a similar oral mild stimulant drug most predominantly associated with people of African descent living in Sweden (irrespective of whether they are Swedish citizens); it was banned outright in the late 1980s. Foreign drugs are banned, it seems, whilst their Swedish equivalents are vigorously defended on an international political stage.

> 'It is salutary to reflect on the outrage expressed about "foreign" drugs, their effects on individuals and society (whether hard or soft) and the need to stem the threatening flood and the lack of sympathy for another group of countries trying to do the same thing with a Swedish "national" drug.'
>
> (Gould 1996)

Therefore, where Sweden aspires towards a 'drug-free society', 'drug' is understood to mean a *foreign* substance not seen to be inherently Swedish. In contrast to the moral panic concerning foreign drugs, Sweden insists on being allowed to maintain its national drugs, perhaps driven by something of an unspoken fear of emasculation – alcohol and snus both tied in heavily with Swedish models of normative masculinity – in spite of snus being unacceptable in the EU of which Sweden is a member state. Swedish drugs have their places in the Swedish People's Home since, it seems, they are understood to be better than others.

Summary: pathologisation and demonisation of drugs and people who use them

People who use drugs are heavily stigmatised in Sweden. They are stigmatised through conflationary and generalising constructions, driven in no small part by the addiction-as-disease model of understanding, with people who use drugs seen to be sick, helpless, dangerous, lying, and manipulative – particularly people with drug dependencies (though it should be stressed that whether people actually have what may be perceived to be a drug dependency or not is somewhat moot given that drug use is so heavily conflated). This constructed disease results in people who use drugs being commonly seen as both infantile – unable to exercise agency and self-determination – and criminal, unpredictable, and dangerous, the double-edged stigma of pathology and criminality. The generalisations of people who use drugs are paralleled by crude conflations of the drugs that they use. Drugs are all (unempirically) considered equally 'bad': drugs are bad and so, therefore, are the people who use them. Yet there are certain drugs which escape such labelling as bad, and, for all intents and purposes are not seen to be drugs at all in Sweden. These are alcohol and tobacco (particularly snus), seen to be quintessentially Swedish, inherent facets of Swedish history and culture. Sweden's criminalisation and heavy stigmatisation of various other (un-Swedish) drugs themselves – many of which are arguably less detrimental to the individual, and to wider society, than legal Swedish drugs – has been driven by the same xenophobic and racialised fears that catalysed the introduction of Sweden's legislation criminalising the *use* of drugs. Un-Swedish, alien drugs are not to be welcomed or socially included and integrated into the People's Home, and neither are those who use them.

Many of these understandings – notably the addiction-as-disease model and the arbitrary, capricious, and discriminatory criminalisation and control of certain drugs but not others – are not peculiar to Sweden. What *is* peculiar to Sweden, however, is the understanding that drug use in-and-of-itself is also a disease. Not only are people who use drugs constructed as pathological but so is their drug use, with drug users seen to be vectors transmitting the disease of drug use on to others. There is thus a double pathologisation of people who use drugs in Sweden, and thus an attendant double stigmatisation: people who use drugs have a disease; and their drug use is also a disease.

It is these understandings that have come to so effectively justify the sidelining and silencing of people who use drugs and their organisations, excluding them from debates and discussions that relate to their own lives, which has helped Sweden's establishment of consensus on issues surrounding drugs, discussed in the previous chapter. And these understandings furthermore serve to justify the incarceration and forced treatment of people who use drugs, whose literal social exclusion is seen to be necessary both to protect them from themselves, and additionally to protect society at large from their transmitting their disease of drug use to normatively acceptable non-drug using citizens of Sweden's *folkhemmet.*

Having focussed in the first two chapters on the genealogy of the debates surrounding Sweden's drug legislation and on the discursive backdrop that has framed those debates, I turn my attention in the next chapter to how Swedish drug legislation has come to impact the dynamics of drugs and drug use in Sweden, and the levels and spaces of drug use.

Notes

1 These understandings, constructions, and generalising stereotypes are frequently heavily stigmatising; stigma, specifically hatred and fear of people who use drugs – what may be termed 'drug-userphobia' (INPUD 2015) – is discussed in Chapter 6.

2 Where 'problem drug user' is taken to mean 'injecting drug use or long-duration/regular use of opioids, cocaine and/or amphetamines' (EMCDDA 2009), it should be emphasised that the term 'problematic/problem drug user' is by no means universally accepted or uncontested. This term, along with 'abuser' and 'misuser', is 'often used in an uncritical, disparaging or hostile way', noted to be misleading and universalising (INPUD 2011). Instead, it may be argued that terms like 'problem'/'problematic' drug user should perhaps be taken to provide a reflection of an individual's situation, connoting drug use that has become problematic for a person, not a blanket term generalising all of a 'type' of drug use(r). Terminology, like drug classification, should be more objective, more descriptive, and less vague and open to subjective assumption than this use of 'problematic' or 'problem', in contrast to the taken-for-granted assumptions surrounding addiction-as-disease discourse. Injecting or dependence should not, by default, be defined to be problematic, especially given that many of the harms that may result – both to the individual and to society – in the first place stem from such moralistic problematisation, and criminalisation of drugs and the people who use them, as discussed in Chapter 1 of this book.

3 Dynamics and displacement of Swedish drug use

Though criminalisation of and punitive approaches to drug use continue to be implemented globally, there is little evidence to suggest that these policies have yielded positive results, with it being argued that the 'global war on drugs has failed' (Global Commission on Drug Policy 2011: 4) in its principal ambition of decreasing levels of drug use. In spite of the ongoing popularity of punitive prohibition and criminalisation of drugs and the people who use them, prohibitionism has failed in its principal ambition of curbing or diminishing drug use, failing by its own metrics and standards: estimates[1] point to strikingly high levels of global drug use (UNODC 2011; UNODC 2014).

Despite this, Sweden's criminalisation of the use of drugs outspokenly aims to create a 'drug free society', as well as to send a signal that Sweden does not tolerate drugs or people who use drugs. So far, this book has been concerned with the inception and conception of Sweden's prohibitionist drug legislation, and the discursive backdrops that have informed the adoption of these laws. In this chapter, I am principally interested in the dynamics of Swedish drug use, in whether levels of drug use and the spaces where drugs are bought and sold have been affected by Swedish legislation, and particularly in whether Swedish legislation has succeeded in its utopian, prohibitionist ambition to achieve a society free of problematised, 'un-Swedish' drugs.

I begin with a focus on levels and modes of drug use – which drugs are used, and why. Discussion will then move on to an analysis of the spaces of 'drug scenes' (areas where drugs are bought and sold), and how these have changed over time, with Sweden's capital city of Stockholm serving as a specific case study. Themes of spatial displacement and social exclusion will be central to these discussions.

Which drugs?

Injecting drug use in Sweden is something of an EU anomaly (Boekhout van Solinge 1997): as opposed to heroin, amphetamine – introduced extensively in Sweden in 1938 (UNODC 2006) – is 'the most common illegal intravenous drug in Sweden' (Ljungberg et al. 1991: 892; also see: Hallam 2010; Lenke and Olsson 2002; Norden et al. 2013). Numbers of individuals requiring medical treatment where amphetamine is the primary cause are relatively few in most European states, but make up 34% of drug-related medical admittance in Sweden (EMCDDA 2009). Somewhat similarly to alcohol, amphetamine is seen to be something of a 'traditional' Swedish drug (though without such a long cultural history as alcohol, with panic surrounding amphetamines being peculiar to the mid-late 20th century onwards), with usage peaking in 1959 at 313,000 users, 6.4% of the populace aged 15–64, and subsequently dropping to 25,000, or 0.4% of the populace aged 15–64, by 2000/2003 (UNODC 2006):

> 'Sweden has like a traditional use of amphetamine… we had like problems with it already in the 1940s, 1950s.'
>
> (Interview, IOGT-NTO; Previously RNS)

> 'We have an amphetamine problem that is larger [than heroin]. The drug problem is not about opiates; it is also about opiates, but not only.'
>
> (Interview, RNS)

In contrast to amphetamine, heroin use was not notable in Sweden until the late 1960s, and ecstasy and cocaine are 'of limited importance' (UNODC 2006: 23), with amphetamine possibly acting as competition for the spread of the latter stimulant (Lenke and Olsson 2002). As is the case through Europe, cannabis is the most commonly used illicit substance in Sweden (EMCDDA 2010; UNODC 2006).

Levels of drug use

Overall levels of drug use in Sweden have been historically low (Hallam 2010), as with other phenomena that have catalysed moral panics in Sweden despite historically low levels (sex work being one pertinent example [Levy 2015]). However, though 'overall prevalence remains low, the extent to which this is due to Sweden's drug policy, or to wider social, historical and geographical factors, cannot be easily surmised from the available information' (Hallam 2010: 9). A UNODC (2006) report that emphasises Sweden's 'successful drugs policy' has been criticised as considerably flawed, since it assumes that the correlation between more recent restrictive policy and low prevalence of drug consumption is indicative of causality (Cohen 2006). Drug experimentation is, in fact, argued by the Swedish National Council for Crime Prevention (in UNODC 2006) to have increased amongst young Swedish people through the 1990s, as opposed to diminishing following the criminalisation of drug use in 1988; reported lifetime prevalence for students aged 15–16 rose from 4% in 1989 to 9% in 2001, and then declined to 6% in 2006 (EMCDDA 2010). Furthermore, it seems that recorded drug offences – mostly use and possession offences – have been increasing, with a mean annual increase of 7% noted between 1998 and 2008 (EMCDDA 2008). Though this may only indicate increases in detection, it does not support the argument that the criminalisation of the use of drugs has yielded a decrease in drug use.

Since 1998, Swedish levels of what are defined as 'problem' and injecting drug use have been fairly constant, estimated in 2007 at around 29,513 (EMCDDA 2010).[2] Overall numbers are lower in Sweden than in other states such as the UK, Italy, and Spain (UNODC 2006). However, where few Swedes have tried illicit drugs, the *proportion* of problem drug users amongst overall people who use drugs is high in Sweden. Between one in five and one in six people who use drugs (annual prevalence) is a problem user (UNODC 2006), and so where Sweden boasts low levels of people who use drugs, it 'seems to be less effective in preventing drug users from becoming drug addicts' (UNODC 2006: 51). Problematic terminology aside, it seems that Sweden is less effective at ensuring that drug use does not result in difficulties – what may be termed 'problematic use' – for people who use drugs (Norden et al. 2013). Drug-related deaths in Sweden are argued to be twice the EU mean (Linton 2011), with mortality directly attributable to nonmedical drug use and overdose being 241 in 2008; this is considerably higher than the Netherland's 129 (EMCDDA 2011), in spite of the Netherlands' population being almost 1.8 times larger than Sweden's (the latter being a state to have adopted many harm reduction interventions, the former a state staunchly historically opposed to harm reduction, as is discussed in the next chapter). Indeed, a UK House of Commons examination of Ralf Löfstedt – a senior advisor at Sweden's Ministry of Social Affairs – notes that Sweden has one of the highest fatality rates due to overdose in Europe (Home Affairs Minutes of Evidence 2002).

It therefore seems that where prohibitionist Sweden may claim a low overall number of people who use drugs, these statistics obscure a high drug-related mortality and relatively high proportions of people who use drugs who develop issues with health and wellbeing (Lenke and Olsson 2002), in part reflecting the social exclusion to which people who use drugs are subject in Sweden, and additionally reflecting the dearth of service and healthcare provision for people who use drugs in Sweden, particularly harm reduction and drug-related education programmes. This is discussed principally in Chapters 4 and 6.

> 'Sweden is among the best in the world to prevent young people from taking drugs, and among our young people there are quite low number who really tries or uses… but comparing with other countries… we are not good at taking care of people who really are uses [using] drugs… we have a high number of people who is using more heavy drug who dies in Sweden, compared to other countries.'
>
> (Interview, Politician – The Left Party; Former Drug User)

Despite the fact that the EMCDDA statistics quoted above are calculated using universalised criteria, noting only instances directly attributable to drug consumption, the seemingly high number of drug-related deaths in Sweden was downplayed by a respondent from the Stockholm Police, and additionally by Löfstedt in the above UK House of Commons examination, questioning the comparability of international statistics:

'when it comes to statistics, Sweden has a big problem, we are far too honest with our statistics… if you have a person that has committed suicide under the influence of drugs, you would consider that, in Sweden, as a drug-related death.'

(Interview, Stockholm Police [Narcotics Division Team Leader])

This respondent emphasised that this 'honesty' was not the case in reporting by countries like the Netherlands and other more 'drug liberal' states. 'Sweden's problem' of being 'too honest' thus means that when compared internationally, Sweden's apparently relatively high proportions of problematic drug users and numbers of drug-related deaths are simply explained away and immaterialised.

Levels of alcohol consumption

'Pure alcohol consumption in Sweden is 37% lower than the Eur-A average. Swedes have harmful drinking patterns… as shown by their relatively high mortality from alcohol-related causes.'

(WHO 2004: 2)

As discussed, alcohol is seen to be historically and traditionally rooted in Sweden. Sweden has relatively low but increasing levels of overall alcohol consumption (Rehm et al. 2007).[3] However, in spite of apparently lower alcohol use than other EU states such as the Netherlands and France, levels of liver cirrhosis (and resultant death) are higher in Sweden, both reflecting high levels of irregular, heavy binge drinking (Rehm et al. 2007; WHO 2004), and high levels of domestic production of alcohol, the use of which is relatively clandestine and unmonitored (Van der Giessen and Van Brussel 1996).

Again, global influences and EU membership are seen as threatening to Sweden and Swedish cultural traditions: 'European drinking' (Boekhout van Solinge 1997), typified by states such as France, whose drinking patterns are 'less detrimental' than those of Sweden, but where overall alcohol consumption in 2002 was almost 50% higher (Rehm et al. 2007), are seen to pose particular risk, with a fear of introducing habits of regular drinking throughout the week, compounding the traditional Swedish weekly binge drinking I observed throughout fieldwork.

'the problem now is that Sweden has a tradition of drinking strong liquor, like vodka, you know, like, a lot… and drinking really much, a lot during the weekends, and now also adopting to, like Mediterranean countries and their traditions. So, Swedes, now, start to drink wine during the weeks as well.'

(Interview, IOGT-NTO; Previously RNS)

'[With bag in box wine] you take a glass… constantly, like the French people, always a little bit [drunk], you know, red wine nose, all day long, so, it has changed.'

(Interview, Stockholm Police [Narcotics Division Team Leader])

Swedish legislation, then, aiming to prevent – or at least reduce – consumption of drugs and alcohol cannot be said to have been successful in achieving its prohibitionist ambitions and aims. The same must be said of the harms directly associated with the use of psychoactive drugs (including alcohol), which have not been reduced through Sweden's legislation and policy; quite the opposite, those who use drugs in Sweden (including alcohol) are at increased risk of experiencing difficulties and harms associated with their use of drugs and/or alcohol.

For the remainder of this chapter, I now turn my attention to the spaces and dynamics of Sweden's drug scenes, that is, areas where drugs are and have historically been bought, sold, and used. I will examine Sweden's capital city, Stockholm, as a case study illustrating patterns in Sweden's spatial enforcement of drug laws and policies.

Spaces: public drug scenes

Making contact

Location, infrastructure, and transport have influenced where drug scenes have developed in Stockholm. The city's most established public drug scene, where people buy and sell drugs, is Sergels Torg (see Figures 3.1 and 3.2), a large square in the centre of the city, commonly referred to as *Plattan* (The Plate/Slab). One of the exits of Stockholm's T-Centralen Central subway station opens onto the square; other drug scenes were noted by respondents to have developed in the suburban transport hubs of Tensta, Rinkeby, Gullmarsplan, and Liljeholmen.

> 'It's the same, it's the bus, it's the subway... it's very much about communication.'
>
> (Interview, RFHL)

A respondent from the Stockholm Police Narcotics Division (Interview, 2009) noted that different drugs are dealt in different parts of Stockholm, and additionally are associated with different groups. *Plattan* is a centre for cannabis, various depressant drugs, and pills (Subutex and benzodiazepines such as diazepam [Valium]). Amphetamine is reportedly mainly dealt in the southern suburbs and the central island of Södermalm, and additionally to some extent in the Central Station and *Plattan*. Cannabis is dealt all over the city, with heroin mostly sold in western and southern suburbs. Tying in with Sweden's association of certain drugs with certain 'un-Swedish' communities and practices (discussed in Chapter 1), the same police officer respondent racialised and classified the drug market during interview, and generalised cannabis selling to be mostly associated with North African organisations originating from states such as Libya, Morocco, and Tunisia; heroin and cocaine were felt to be sold by West African organisations, mostly from Gambia, Senegal, and The Ivory Coast; amphetamine distribution – much in line with its understanding as a culturally Swedish drug – was thought to be dominated by Swedes and people from Poland.

Figure 3.1 Sergels Torg square, also known as *Plattan*, in the centre of Stockholm

Figure 3.2 Map of Central Stockholm highlighting public drug buying and selling areas (*Plattan*) and street-based sex work (*Malmskillnadsgatan*)

A displacement of drug dealing and of people who use drugs

There is scant empirical evidence that prohibitionist legislation has resulted in a decline of levels of drug use in Sweden. Laws and discourse seem instead to have been deliberately favoured as a means with which to achieve a displacement and disruption of public drug use and drug scenes, removing people who use drugs from visible space. In Stockholm, police policies have resulted in a displacement of drug dealing from *Plattan* to more clandestine and diffuse suburban spaces of the city. Focus through the 1970s had moved on from a treatment of 'drug victims' and a concentration on policing drug syndicates, to policing and displacement of street drug dealers and people who use drugs themselves (Anker 2007; Lenke and Olsson 2002). Following from the introduction of this process of focussing on street-based drug dealers and people who use drugs, the centre of Stockholm is periodically cleansed of drug buying, selling, and those who use drugs, with police sweeps of *Plattan* (see Figure 3.1) resulting in the formation of several other drug scenes:

> 'in my mind, one of the important parts of drug strategy is to try to avoid what you call open drug scenes. So this is one of the objectives in our strategy.'
>
> (Interview, Senior Advisor – Ministry of Social Affairs)

> 'That idea [of spatial displacement] is still very present in Sweden. You know in Stockholm we have this Sergels Torg, *Plattan*: always with maybe five years between them, the police make sweeps and clean the Sergels Torg from drug users and drug dealers. And the only effect this police action has done is that ten years ago we had one open drug scene. And that was Sergels Torg. Now we have five open drug scenes in the city.'
>
> (Interview, RFHL)

Cellular phones and the rise in the internet have facilitated this more dispersed drug scene, and this makes it difficult to clearly demonstrate whether legislation and policy, or technological development, has been instrumental in dictating spatial shifting. This has not only impacted the dynamics of drug buying and selling, but also other informal markets, as per the second quotation below: sex work in Sweden moved into increasingly clandestine space following the criminalisation of the purchase of sex and additionally the increasing popularity of mobile telephones and the internet after 1999; the Swedish criminalisation of the purchase of sex – and its use as a strategy for displacing street-based sex work – is discussed in greater detail below.

> 'Because of the police being very active in those areas, and the drug trade has moved to [the] suburbs of Stockholm, so you have suburbs like Gullmarsplan and Rinkeby, Tensta… with the mobile phone, and everything then, they just SMS each other, or call, and then meet up in an apartment, so it's not very obvious where the action is.'
>
> (Interview, IOGT-NTO; Previously RNS)

Figure 3.3 Police presence in *Plattan*, around the T-Centralen subway station exit

> 'Internet has had that effect on everything [surrounding sex work] as well, also with the drug selling and buying, and everything is now very easy with internet as a tool, and also mobile phones and you know. So, I think that would have happened anyway, even if you hadn't had the, the law.'
>
> (ibid.)

Owing to the criminalisation of the very use of drugs, drug use – in addition to drug buying and selling – has been displaced into more clandestine locales. Authorities' harassment and displacement of people who use drugs has severe health implications for people who use drugs, leading to a rushing during injection and/or other drug use, unhygienic injecting, difficulties in clearly establishing the amount of drug used prior to use, hasty discarding of injection paraphernalia, and the sharing of drug paraphernalia, such as needles, syringes, and straws for snorting or smoking.

> '1969 you probably could do that [use drugs in public] for a couple of hours before the police came. Today you might, could do it for ten minutes before the police comes.'
>
> (Interview, RFHL, Drug User)

There are no supervised drug consumption rooms/facilities in Sweden, as opposed to Sweden's neighbour Norway, for example, and respondents from Swedish drug user rights organisation *Svenska Brukarföreningen* and RFHL noted people injecting in parks, garages, communal residential stairwells, and public toilets.

These spaces are far from safe, with 'semi-public' environments associated with increased risks to health and wellbeing, particularly associated with risk of the transmission of blood-borne infections (Rhodes 2006). These spaces are additionally subject to police violence, abuse, and attention, which is explored further in Chapter 6.

> 'They're shooting up in public toilets and things like that... which causes great much irritation at [for] people... you should provide kind of injection rooms where they can go, and take a fix without irritating anyone.'
>
> (Interview, RFHL, Drug User)

Compulsory treatment of people who use drugs, with its attendant periods of medicalised incarceration of people with drug dependencies, should also be understood in this context of Swedish projects of displacement and cleansing and moralising of the public arena, another mechanism of spatial policing used to contain and remove groups who are constructed as being deviant, a threat to Sweden's aspirations of a normative, rational, modern drug-free Swedish society and a blight on the image of Swedish *folkhemmet*, the People's Home.

> 'A lot of money was spent of course on the building prisons, of locking people in. We also had this new legislation in the... social welfare system, we have a law that makes it possible to lock people in for six months because they are drug addicts.'
>
> (Interview, Chair of RFHL)

Treatment and wellbeing of people who use drugs seems secondary, then, to their containment, with laws functioning as 'a method by which they can be tidied away' (Gould 1989: 740): public order and the moral cleanliness of the public spaces of the People's Home are apparently of primary concern to law enforcement.

> 'They should be on treatment programmes, rehab programmes or whatever. But we use, instead, the money to put them into jail.'
>
> (Interview, Chair of RFHL)

Broader projects of displacement and social engineering

Sweden's projects of displacement are not limited to the spatial where, as discussed in the previous chapter, people who use drugs have been figuratively displaced and distanced – through their being silenced and excluded – in the context of political debate relating to drugs and drug policies. Nor are Sweden's displacements of marginalised communities limited to the contemporary displacing of people who use drugs from public space and areas of civil society. Sweden has a long history of spatially displacing marginalised communities, of containing and controlling the movements of those deemed to pose a threat to the normative safety of the

Swedish *folkhemmet*, the People's Home. As discussed in this book's Introduction, the 19th and 20th centuries in Sweden were marked by the use of numerous pieces of legislation as means with which to control people who use drugs and alcohol, sex workers, women, the homeless, and immigrants. Vagrancy, venereal disease, and HIV/AIDS legislation (under the auspices of contagious disease legislation) have all been used, variously or simultaneously, to displace marginalised communities (Baldwin 1999; Baldwin 2005; Blom 2007; Henriksson and Ytterberg 1992; Hubbard et al. 2007a; Svanström 2006). As I have endeavoured to stress, Sweden's displacement of people who use drugs must therefore be seen in the context of a history of social engineering and spatial discipline, with visible drug use serving as an unwanted reminder that an aspiration towards a clean and disciplined *folkhemmet* has failed.

> 'We have this… faith, trust and faith also, in social engineering.'
>
> (Interview, RFHL)

> 'We haven't really made up with our history when it comes to the picture of ourselves as the strong Arian woman and man, and we're supposed to be perfect… we are a very nice, clean country, and we supposed to have no drug addicts here.'
>
> (ibid.)

> 'You want to get rid of the drug addicts in cities, where you don't want to meet them in the streets, you don't want to see them, you know, at Sergels Torg, *Plattan*; they're dirty, probably dangerous.'
>
> (Interview, RFHL, Drug User)

> 'The political view is Sweden should be [a] drug-free society, and if you… want a drug-free society, you don't want drug users. So just put them away from the society.'
>
> (Interview, *Svenska Brukarföreningen* Stockholm Coordinator; Former Drug User)

Sweden's 1999 sex purchase law has been strikingly similar to Sweden's criminalisation of the use of drugs, both in terms of its parallel focus on entirely *eliminating demand* through criminalising the *purchase* of sex (as the *use* of drugs is criminalised in attempt to entirely *eliminate* drugs from Sweden), but additionally in terms of how the legislation has come to be employed, how it has come to be realised as policy. The *sexköpslagen* legislation was introduced in the context of similarly racialised, xenophobic, and HIV-related panics to those that surrounded the criminalisation of the use of drugs (Gould 2001; Kulick 2003; Kulick 2005; Levy 2015), and following the introduction of the criminalisation of the purchase of sex, this legislation has been used with considerable similarity to how Sweden's drug legislation has been deployed: to displace sex workers from public space. Following the introduction of the law, 7 million Swedish krona were spent on policing, with considerable sums spent on CCTV around areas of street-based sex work (Danna 2012; Hubbard et al. 2007b), with the police focussing heavily on these public areas of sex work in Sweden's major cities (Clausen 2007; Danna 2012; Kulick 2003). And because clients are increasingly unwilling to buy sex in public spaces due to their being criminalised, there has been 'a spatial switching from street to off-street, with much more sex work now occurring in hidden sectors which are not monitored by the police' (Hubbard et al. 2007a: 20). As with previous legislation (vagrancy; communicable disease; venereal; eugenic sterilisation policies, and so forth) used in the 19th and 20th centuries, the sex purchase law has been applied selectively, with marked similarity to the Swedish drug legislation that came into being a decade beforehand:

> 'of course there is a gradual progression in cleaning public spaces… that is clearly very evident'.
>
> (Interview, Senior Advisor Regarding Prostitution – National Board of Health and Welfare [*Socialstyrelsen*])

> 'Stockholm has a police unit who works with zero tolerance. And they [have] done that when it comes to drug users, homelessness, and prostitution.'
>
> (Interview, Social Worker, Malmö Prostitution Unit I)

The abovementioned displacements of sex workers from areas of street-based sex work have gone hand-in-hand with police-orchestrated evictions from residential premises, as well as the police raiding sex workers' hotel rooms, and informing hotels and venues that specific individuals are selling sex from their premises, thus enacting yet more displacements and disruptions (Danna 2012; Kulick 2003; Levy 2015; Östergren 2004; Östergren and Dodillet 2011). And Sweden has not only displaced sex workers intranationally/domestically, but internationally also, through deportations of migrant sex workers (Danna 2012; Levy 2015; Levy and Jakobsson 2013; Östergren and Dodillet 2011). Such displacements – whether of sex work, or of drug use – have resulted in increasing difficulties for affected communities, problematising outreach, healthcare and service provision access, and increasing danger of violence, abuse, and social exclusion (Clausen 2007; Hubbard et al. 2007b; Kilvington et al. 2001; Kulick 2003; Levy 2015; *Socialstyrelsen* [National Board of Health and Welfare] 2008). I argue in the following chapter that this exacerbation of the harms which may be associated with drug use (and sex work) should not be regarded as an unintended side-effect of Sweden's prohibitionist, criminalising legislation, but rather as a deliberate consequence. Indeed, I argue that Sweden actively aims to exacerbate the difficulties that people who use drugs experience in order to discourage drug use (as is also the case with Sweden's efforts to exacerbate the difficulties that can surround sex work in order to (unsuccessfully) incentivise people to cease selling sex [Levy 2015]). I term these policies Sweden's 'harm exacerbation' policies, in contradistinction to harm reduction interventions.

Summary: drug difficulties, displacement, containment, and control

Which drugs are used, and how they are used, have been very much culturally determined in Sweden. Sweden has been something of an outlier in terms of injecting drug use, with historically normalised use of amphetamines informing ongoing high prevalence of amphetamine stimulant use and injecting amphetamine use, as opposed to opiates being the principal injected drug, as is the case in many other European states. Amphetamines are not the only popular drug in Sweden: alongside Sweden's robust construction of illicit drugs as deviant and problematic, patterns of alcohol consumption and alcohol acceptability are informed by alcohol's being perceived as culturally Swedish, important, and normative, not really seen to be a drug at all – as discussed in the previous chapter. Yet alcohol is very much used by Swedes as a psychoactive drug, with patterns of alcohol use being driven by a desire for intoxication: Swedes drink to get drunk, and this has informed a culture of binge drinking and resultant high levels of liver cirrhosis.

As I hope to have made clear though, Sweden's drug-free aspirations should be seen to only focus on drugs constructed to be problematic, drugs seen as threatening to destabilise an ordered and rational *folkhemmet*. But Sweden's ambition to create a society free of problematised drugs through prohibitionist, repressive legislation has been a failure. Levels of illicit drug use are admittedly low in Sweden, but they have always been so and there are no data suggesting that the Swedish model on drugs has led to low levels of drug use. Sweden cannot boast that its legislation has been responsible for decreasing levels of drug use, as was intended.

Instead, Swedish prohibitionist drug legislation has been used as a lens through which to police and morally cleanse public space, to displace people who use drugs from civil society and in so doing, to aesthetically sanitise public areas. This displacement should be seen as a facet of a broader project of Swedish modernity, social engineering, and spatial cleansing, as a part of Sweden's history of containing and controlling groups constructed as being deviant and disruptive. Vagrancy legislation, contagious and venereal disease legislation, and the criminalisation of the purchase of sex have all been used at various times as means with which to displace and contain what is seen to be an aesthetic blight and nuisance of marginalised, problematised communities, the presence of whom threatens to highlight Sweden's failure in establishing an ordered, clean, and modern *folkhemmet*; Sweden's drug legislation must be understood similarly.

Despite low levels of drug use in Sweden, those who choose to use drugs appear to suffer greater drug-related harms than in other states, with levels of overdose-related mortality, for example, being higher in Sweden and, as is discussed in greater detail in Chapter 6, other drug-related harms are higher in Sweden too. Social exclusion and denial of appropriate and comprehensive healthcare and service provision are known to contribute to negative impacts upon the health of people who use drugs. It is the Swedish model on service provision for people who use drugs that I now turn my attention to in the following two chapters.

Notes

1 People who use drugs make up clandestine groups due to criminalisation, stigmatisation, and marginalisation. This results in difficulties in sampling and estimating population sizes and prevalences (Bluthenthal et al. 2000; Degenhardt and Hall 2012).
2 I should reemphasise that I have considerable problems with the EMCDDA's (and others') arbitrary definition of 'problem' drug use. This is discussed in greater detail in the endnotes of the previous chapter.
3 This would apply to *measurable* alcohol consumption, as opposed to alcohol produced illegally in people's homes.

4 Service provision and harm reduction

In this chapter, I focus on how Swedish understandings and constructions of drugs and people who use drugs have fed through into the understandings and approaches of Swedish service and healthcare providers. Particularly, this chapter focusses on how Sweden's prohibitionist discourses have impacted service provision for people who use drugs, and this chapter will concentrate on what services are available, and which are absent.

I also focus to some extent on geographical variation within Sweden, where various discourses and municipal independence have affected what services people who use drugs have access to, and where. Harm reduction programmes and interventions are a specific area of focus: Sweden's desire to create a drug-free society has markedly impacted how harm reduction is understood, and has also informed which harm reduction services are available for people who use drugs.

Harm reduction

The need for harm reduction

Before moving on to a discussion of Swedish service provision for people who use drugs, it is necessary to elaborate on what harm reduction involves, and why it has come to be advocated as imperative for people who use drugs.

Harms that are associated with drug use are considerable and multitudinous. I should re-stress that these harms are not only associated directly with psychoactive drugs themselves, but are also driven, exacerbated, and created by criminalisation and stigma, as well as by the discrimination and social exclusion they drive. I refer to all these harms collectively as being drug-related: as a result of these drug-related harms, there are estimated to be around 183,000 drug-related deaths globally every year (UNODC 2014). In addition to the risk of blood-borne infections like HIV and hepatitis C (both are discussed further below) which is associated with the sharing of injection paraphernalia, adverse outcomes of drug use – whether due to the use of the drug in-and-of itself, or whether due to the harms that result from prohibition, criminalisation, and a lack of harm reduction interventions – include toxicity and overdoses; development of dependence;[1] impacts of intoxication (such as traffic accidents, violence, accidental injury); and adverse impacts upon health and mental health from sustained use (Degenhardt and Hall 2012; also see Darke and Hall 2003). Harms are not confined to the individual: substantial financial costs result from 'wars against drugs' and prohibitive policies, with additional social costs of healthcare and social issues (Nutt et al. 2010; UNODC 2011).

Globally, 12.7 million people are estimated to be injecting drug users (UNODC 2014). The spread of blood-borne infections like hepatitis C and HIV has been driven in many regions and contexts by the sharing of injection paraphernalia and equipment, which frequently occurs due to difficulties in obtaining sterile injecting equipment and due to repressive legislative environments, which result in multitudinous barriers to using drugs more safely and hygienically, and to accessing service and healthcare provision (for example see Advisory Council on the Misuse of Drugs 2009; Degenhardt and Hall 2012; Drucker et al. 1998; Gibson et al. 1999; Global Commission on Drug Policy 2012; Rhodes et al. 2002; WHO 2007). The UNODC (2011) estimate that 17.9% of people who inject drugs (2.8 million) are living with HIV.[2] Hepatitis C is even more striking in prevalence, considered the 'most important infectious disease affecting those who inject drugs' (Health Protection Agency et al. 2007) with 45.2% to 55.3% – around 8 million – of people who inject drugs believed to be living with hepatitis C (UNODC 2011),[3] accounting for the majority of the infection's global spread (Rhodes et al. 2004). As with other blood-borne infections like HIV, transmission of hepatitis C is facilitated through needle sharing, but hepatitis C can additionally be transmitted through the sharing of other injection paraphernalia and, as a result, the probability and incidence of hepatitis C transmission is substantially higher than that of HIV, which is less likely to be spread through sharing of other paraphernalia (Advisory Council on the Misuse of Drugs 2009; Nelson et al. 2011; Rhodes et al. 2004).

Harm reduction strategies

With prohibition- and criminalisation-driven harms argued to be increasing globally, the need to adopt a public health and harm reduction perspective in order to avoid further cost and harm is emphasised (International Federation of Red Cross and Red Crescent Societies 2003; WHO 2005a). It is emphasised that law enforcement and harm reduction are not mutually exclusive (Stevens et al. 2010), and it is argued that '(l)aw enforcement efforts should focus not on reducing drug markets *per se* but rather on reducing their harms' (Global Commission on Drug Policy 2011). Harm reduction interventions are defined by Harm Reduction International as follows:

> 'Harm reduction refers to policies, programmes and practices that aim to reduce the harms associated with the use of psychoactive drugs in people unable or unwilling to stop. The defining features are the focus on the prevention of harm, rather than on the prevention of drug use itself, and the focus on people who continue to use drugs.'
>
> (Harm Reduction International n.d.)

Reducing the avoidable harms which may be associated with drug use, reducing the likelihood of transmission of blood-borne infections, and providing healthcare to people who use drugs, in particular to those who inject, may be achieved by (for example see Advisory Council on the Misuse of Drugs 2009; Drucker et al. 1998; Gibson et al. 1999; Hurley et al. 1997; Stimson 1989; Tammi 2005a; WHO 2004b; WHO UNODC UNAIDS 2009) decreasing needle sharing (through needle/syringe programmes, needle/syringe vending machines, and pharmacy provision), bleach and paraphernalia distribution, drug content testing (such as is available in the Netherlands), straw (for snorting) provision, foil (for smoking drugs like heroin and crystal methamphetamine) provision, street-based outreach work, referral, disseminating information, education/peer education regarding risk behaviours (including sex education), condom provision, counselling and testing services, legal and social services, stigma reduction programmes, naloxone as part of overdose prevention work, and opiate substitution therapy.[4]

Some harm reduction discourse deliberately positions itself neutrally (International Federation of Red Cross and Red Crescent Societies 2003; Tammi and Hurme 2006), differing from a prohibitionist approach in that it does not aspire to a reduction of drug use (Drucker et al. 1998). Though prohibitionism is demonstrated to increase the harms surrounding drug use – and is thus seemingly incompatible with a harm reduction philosophy – harm reduction and prohibitionism are not *necessarily* mutually exclusive: many people currently use drugs, and harm reduction should therefore be deployed to mitigate the surrounding harms within current (arguably harmful) legislative frameworks (Tammi 2005a; UNODC 2008). I should reemphasise (again and again!), however, that it is prohibition and criminalisation that themselves create, drive, and exacerbate the vast majority of those very harms that harm reduction services aim to reduce and mitigate.

Opposition to harm reduction

> 'All of the harm reduction principles – individualism, inclusion, pragmatism and emancipation – resonate extremely well with the moral sensibilities of our contemporary societies. Ever fewer people would oppose them as general principles, unlike those of collectivism, exclusion, dogmatism, and paternalism.'
>
> (Tammi and Hurme 2006: 4)

Prohibitionist 'war on drugs' discourse – and the laws and policies that result – serves to hinder harm reduction measures, efforts designed to reduce the harms (notably the transmission of blood-borne infections such as HIV) that may be associated with drug use (Global Commission on Drug Policy 2011; Global Commission on Drug Policy 2012), all for fear that these programmes would encourage and/or facilitate the unwanted and moralised activity of drug use.[5] As a result of prohibitionist narrative and concerns surrounding harm reduction, healthcare initiatives for drug users are frequently aborted and/or withheld (Tammi 2005a). Most people who inject drugs do not have access to harm reduction programmes, service provision, or medical treatment; as the Global

Commission on Drug Policy recently reported (2012: 2; also see Mathers et al. 2010), 'a number of specific countries, including the US, Russia and Thailand [and, as is the focus of this chapter, Sweden], ignore scientific evidence and World Health Organization recommendations and resist the implementation of evidence-based HIV prevention programs – with devastating consequences'.

Modes of facilitating safer drug use are frequently opposed where they appear to undermine prohibitionist messages (Des Jarlais 1995), and/or because they are seen to facilitate and endorse drug use (Hedrich et al. 2010; Hurley et al. 1997; Rhodes 2006). Harm reduction programmes are therefore often not assessed on their merits, but instead in the context of consistency with cultural and social traditions (Des Jarlais 1995), with the established rhetoric of prohibition, criminalisation, and stigmatisation of drug use. A politicisation of research can further ideological ends and discredit empirical analyses, to the detriment of pragmatic, health- and evidence-orientated policies.

> '[M]ethods used to discredit some research have become more diverse and have included funding seemingly independent scientific organizations, quasi-journalist outlets and public relations firms, and lobbying for political appointments to promote special interests.'
>
> (Kerr and Wood 2008: 964)

> 'The war on drugs has also led to a policy distortion whereby evidence-based addiction treatment and public health measures have been downplayed or ignored.'
>
> (Global Commission on Drug Policy 2012: 2)

And so, despite the fact that harm reduction interventions have resonated well with the sensibilities of some states that ostensibly prioritise the individual freedoms of their citizens, harm reduction is seen in Sweden to be in total diametric opposition to Sweden's desire to create a drug-free society (Tammi and Hurme 2006); indeed, in Sweden harm reduction is argued to endorse and encourage drug use. Even the term 'harm reduction' is seen to be undesirable and misleading, with drug use in-and-of-itself constructed as a form of harm to be opposed and abolished; the only way to reduce harm, it is argued, is to abolish drug use entirely. In other words, it is felt that there is no *point* in *reducing* this harm; instead, one has to *eliminate* the harm, characterised very crudely here as drug use, in-and-of-itself.

All of this should be seen in a context of Swedish concern surrounding foreign influence, concern which notably informed the debates prior to the criminalisation of the use of drugs, where harm reduction – and its attendant discourses of prioritising health and human rights over criminalisation, social exclusion, and control – is seen as yet another alien discourse threatening to subvert the normative Swedish nation state; as Gould (2005: 82) notes, there is a fear that '[n]ot only would alien drugs flood into the country but also alien ideas such as *harm reduction* and *decriminalisation*'.

> 'Sweden is working for the UN not to even use the phrase "harm reduction", because in Sweden "harm reduction" is something bad.'
>
> (Interview, *Svenska Brukarföreningen* Stockholm Coordinator; Former Drug User)

> 'In the debate… we can't call it harm reduction. Because RNS and FMN and their political friends have banned the words.'
>
> (Interview, RFHL)

Opposition to drug-related harm reduction is strong in Sweden, unlike other Scandinavian states such as Finland and Norway, which have drug consumption rooms and widespread access to sterile needles and injection paraphernalia. The term 'harm reduction' does not appear on Sweden's 'National Action Plan on Drugs (2006–10)', which instead outlines a restrictive discourse (EMCDDA 2010). Far from pragmatic and productive, harm reduction interventions are seen in Sweden to be a permissive step in the direction of endorsement and liberalism, seen even to be a step toward 'handing out a lot of drugs', as per the below quotation from a representative of the Swedish police. The focus is not on improving the lives of people who use drugs through mitigating the harms which may be associated with their drug use, but instead on helping (or forcing) a cessation of drug use, a policy 'fixated on abstinence' (Baldwin 2005: 154).

> 'The thing that I fear with harm reduction is that you take harm reduction to a level where you start to hand out a lot of drugs.'
>
> (Interview, Stockholm Police [Narcotics Division Team Leader])

> 'I believe that we should help a person get drug-free, not to help them use safer or anything, because if we say… we shouldn't have them [drugs] in our society, then why should we… teach people how to use them?'
>
> (Interview, IOGT-NTO; Previously RNS)

> 'If they in any way help drug users, they think that is the same thing as if they are saying it's okay to take drugs.'
>
> (Interview, *Svenska Brukarföreningen* Stockholm Coordinator; Former Drug User)

> 'We have our policy, Sweden the land of no narcotics… and if we allow harm reduction, [it is thought that] we are accepting that we have drugs in our country.'
>
> (Interview, RFHL)

> 'They say that harm reduction is a conflict to the restrictive drug policy.'
>
> (Interview, Chair and Founder of *Svenska Brukarföreningen*)

Needle and syringe programmes

Opposition to needle and syringe programmes

As discussed earlier in this chapter, needle exchanges and needle and syringe programmes are well-known and have been widely demonstrated to decrease risk behaviour and transmission of blood-borne infections amongst people who inject drugs, tallying with a study of one of Sweden's two needle exchanges, which demonstrated positive outcomes and 'substantial changes in risk behaviour' (Ljungberg et al. 1991: 895; also see Henriksson and Ytterberg 1992).

> 'There is clear research. This [opposition to needle and syringe programmes] is bullshit… we have clear evidence, it is clear, what is going on is absolutely unacceptable, that people are playing with, you know, some moralistic anxieties.'
>
> (Interview, Swedish Institute for Communicable Disease Control; Previously National Coordinator for HIV and STI Prevention)

> 'It's been evaluated, you can clearly see it, that in the areas where they actually had the needle exchange you have less people who got infected by HIV, and you certainly got much less people that got infected by hepatitis. This can be proven. So there is no doubt about it.'
>
> (ibid.)

However, such interventions have been opposed repeatedly and internationally, fed by concerns that needle and syringe programmes 'might exacerbate illicit drug use' (WHO 2004a: 8; also see Stimson 1989), may increase injection frequency, needle sharing with other people who inject drugs, numbers of publicly discarded needles, and may serve as a disincentive for people who use drugs to cease their drug use, all of which have resulted in opposition to needle and syringe programmes (WHO 2004a).[6] There has, though, been no convincing empirical evidence justifying these concerns (see WHO 2004a for a review of available evidence), or justifying similar concerns raised regarding safe drug consumption rooms, for that matter (Hedrich et al. 2010).[7]

And so distributing sterile injection paraphernalia is seen as threatening to Sweden's 'traditional narcotics policy' (Ljungberg et al. 1991); there has been strong opposition – politically and in civil society – to the establishment of needle and syringe programmes in Sweden (Anker 2007; Henriksson and Ytterberg 1992) with the medical profession 'accused of attempting to medicalise the drug issue' when campaigning for the establishment of needle and syringe programmes (Tammi 2005b: 387). Despite considerable evidence and scientific consensus to the contrary, key respondents argued that needle and syringe programmes have no empirically demonstrable impact in preventing transmissible blood-borne infections or in improving the health of people who use drugs.

> 'I'm sick and tired of the debate around needle exchange… I don't think it [needle exchange] does much harm, I don't think it does much good either.'
>
> (Interview, Psychiatrist working with drug addiction; Previously RNS)

> 'It [needle exchange] doesn't help. It's never proven to help anything. It maybe, just *maybe*, it doesn't do much harm… There's absolutely no scientific proof anywhere in the world that needle exchange prevents the spreading of hepatitis. That, nobody could argue that. You could argue that there's some small scientific evidence for HIV being prevented. But I think that could be questioned strongly.'
>
> (Interview, RNS)

> 'If science would show that it has an impact on HIV and those kind of things, or HIV, then I [would] think that's okay.'
>
> (Interview, IOGT-NTO; Previously RNS)

Assertions of needle and syringe programmes' lack of efficacy are made by influential groups in Sweden such as RNS, with stakeholders seemingly 'seeking to cloud the science specific to the prevention of HIV' (Kerr and Wood 2008: 964) and other infections. The publication of a paper by Swedish authors (Käll et al. 2007), one of whom is a previous member of RNS, claiming that WHO support of needle and syringe programmes is not empirically justified has been specifically criticised as an example of a 'new and worrisome trend… the creation of internet sites posing as open-access, peer-reviewed scientific journals' (Kerr and Wood 2008: 964).

> 'This happens in the world of [the] internet, that these studies pop up and pop up. People who don't know about research will, you know, say "Ah, this is research", and they have no idea whether it's good or not.'
>
> (Interview, Swedish Institute for Communicable Disease Control; Previously National Coordinator for HIV and STI Prevention)

> 'RNS and other organisations and some politicians, [claim] that there are no evidence, there are no facts showing that the needle exchange programmes save lives.'
>
> (Interview, Chair of RFHL)

In addition to contesting the effectiveness of needle and syringe programmes, provision of sterile needles was thought by key respondents to encourage people to begin *using* drugs, and drug use is thought to be legitimised and endorsed through the provision of tools with which to use drugs safely.

> 'Say that if you give free needles, you also says it's okay, you can go on and take drugs. So instead, you need to help them, take them from the drugs instead.'
>
> (Interview, Politician – Social Democrats)

> '[It is thought that] if young people see that they can get free needles, then they decide "Oh, I will start with the drugs."'
>
> (Interview, *Svenska Brukarföreningen* Stockholm Coordinator; Former Drug User)

> 'They have some kind of idea that if you get a needle, a clean needle or syringe, it becomes [creates] more drug addicts... [They think] the needle, the syringe is the main reason that there are so many drug addicts.'
>
> (Interview, *Svenska Brukarföreningen*; Former Drug User)

In interview, little distinction was made by a Narcotics Division Team Leader between the provision of sterile injection equipment and the outright provision of drugs, the former seen to be a dangerous step towards the latter:

> 'I think that the worry is, if the first step is to give them free needles, is the next step to give them free drugs. Because where is the difference?'
>
> (Interview, Stockholm Police [Narcotics Division Team Leader])

Needle and syringe programmes are thought in Sweden to allow and encourage people who use drugs to continue in their drug use (Henriksson and Ytterberg 1992). Giving people who use drugs needles is seen to facilitate an activity that has been criminalised – the use of drugs – conflicting with Sweden's staunchly prohibitionist aspiration. To reiterate: the focus is entirely on stopping, disincentivising, and/or preventing people from using drugs, with no prioritisation at all whatsoever of the prevention of the transmission of blood-borne infections or of the reduction of drug-related harm through the provision of sterile drug using paraphernalia.

> 'If you have a drug-free society as an overall objective... on one hand say that you shouldn't use drugs, on the other hand you give the equipment necessary to use drugs. That's not logical, connected.'
>
> (Interview, Senior Advisor – Ministry of Social Affairs)

> 'Obviously if you give people needles and say "here's a needle for you to use", then you're not fighting drugs. You're going the other way with that.'
>
> (Interview, RNS)

> 'Why should we give people needles, and that stuff, if it's illegal to use it [drugs]?'
>
> (Interview, Founder of KRIS)

> 'I don't think people should take drugs... if this person don't already have hepatitis or HIV I'm happy, but at the same time, I mean, if they have this needle exchange, and can keep going for two years more, because of this, I can't see why it's good.'
>
> (Interview, National Coordinator Against Trafficking and Prostitution)

'Giving someone a clean needle is like saying "Go on with your heroin abuse: use", and that needle can help that person to kill himself, die from an overdose.'

(Interview, IOGT-NTO; Previously RNS)

'If somebody would show me that that [needle provision] would help people to get drug-free and healthy and we would have less drug problem in our society, by [due to] needle exchange, then I would be totally for it.'

(Interview, IOGT-NTO; Previously RNS)

In Sweden, needle and syringe programmes are not engaged with as a facet of a wider infrastructure of service provision; they are simply compared unfavourably to other blood-borne infection prevention initiatives, such as testing and counselling, essentially as either/or alternatives (see Amundsen et al. 2003). Indeed, there is concern that a focus on harm reduction will serve to sideline these preferred strategies, as opposed to complementing them.

'I think if you have this kind of harm reduction… thinking, I think you can forget a lot of other things. You can make it easy. You say you provide the prostitutes with kits, or you provide the drug addict with a needle… you say instead of talking about stop[ping] with the drug abuse, we give them needles.'

(Interview, National Coordinator Against Trafficking and Prostitution)

'That's the main problem with harm reduction… this could be… seen as very simple… cheap solutions to a complicated problem.'

(Interview, Senior Advisor – Ministry of Social Affairs)

'The problem is that you isolate the other thing [in engaging only with one type of service provision out of context]… and you can't see how they connect. And that's the same with the needle exchange. You can't see how the needle exchange connects with the treatment.'

(Interview, Social Worker, Malmö Prostitution Unit FAST)

This ignores the fact that the Lund needle and syringe programme in the south of Sweden (for many years, the only two needle and syringe programmes in Sweden operated in the southern region of Skåne, in the cities of Malmö and Lund; this is discussed further below) has functioned in a broader context, where 'for a number of drug users, the syringe exchange has served as an introduction to such treatment efforts' (Ljungberg et al. 1991: 890). Thus, for some people who use drugs accessing these services, 'the syringe exchange has been the introduction to drug rehabilitation and thereby the first step towards a change of the drug habits' (Ljungberg et al. 1991: 895), acting as a 'bridge' to other forms of treatment and assistance (Tammi 2005a).

Key respondents also made arguments negating state responsibility for reducing the harms associated with drug use, emphasising that if individuals are illegally purchasing drugs, they should be expected to buy injection equipment themselves (see Käll et al. 2007) illegally: as discussed below, it is illegal for people who use drugs to buy needles and syringes from shops and pharmacies. In short, respondents argued that it was not the Swedish state's responsibility to provide people who use drugs with safe injection paraphernalia.

> 'If they can afford the drugs I'm sure they can afford the [needles], the equipment is so much cheaper than the drugs.'
>
> (Interview, Psychiatrist working with drug addiction; Previously RNS)

> 'Have them [drug users] buy. If they can afford to buy drugs, they could afford… [to buy] a needle, and take responsibility for it themselves.'
>
> (Interview, RNS)

> 'You [are] like, helping people to use drugs… they could get needles, buy needles by themselves, I don't think that we should help them with that… if you can get drugs, you can get needles too.'
>
> (Interview, Social Worker and Counsellor, Stockholm Prostitution Unit)

Injection paraphernalia availability

As of only 2007, every Swedish municipality has been entitled to open a needle and syringe programme (EMCDDA 2008; UNODC 2006). Yet with such staunch opposition, politicians have remained reluctant to endorse and open new programmes. Municipal independence allows for great variability in terms of which services are available: only two needle and syringe programmes existed for a great many years, both in the southern region of Skåne, in the cities of Malmö and Lund. They were established in 1987 and 1986 respectively, and still exist only on an 'experimental' basis, where 'parliament said that, "okay, we can have these as a pilot study, but we don't want to see it anywhere else in the country"' (Interview, Senior Advisor – Ministry of Social Affairs). A state-sponsored needle and syringe programme recently opened in Stockholm (just subsequent to my fieldwork), having been given approval to open only in 2012 (The Local 2012); as the Swedish Public Health Authority have stressed (*Folkhälsomyndigheten* 2015), more are required than these three centres.

> 'Today we have the right to have needle exchange programmes… Not one, not one part of Sweden has done so.'
>
> (Interview, Chair of RFHL)

> '[It is thought that] if you're a local politician that starts a needle exchange programme, then you [are] pro drugs.'
>
> (Interview, *Svenska Brukarföreningen*; Ex-Partner of Drug User)

'Healthcare is decentralised. So it's up to the Stockholm City Council, or the county council to decide.'

(Interview, Politician – Social Democrats [Former Equality Minister]; Former EU Commissioner)

'It has been recommended that it should be done [needle and syringe programmes should be established], but the responsibility for doing this is not on the national authority, it's on the county councils and municipalities.'

(Interview, Swedish Institute for Communicable Disease Control; Previously National Coordinator for HIV and STI Prevention)

'The leading person in the county council here in Stockholm, she is very much against [needle exchange].'

(Interview, Senior Advisor – Ministry of Social Affairs)

The two needle and syringe programmes are not without their problems, with a lack of anonymity vis-à-vis registration (though anonymity is noted to be granted upon request [Månsson et al. 2000]) argued to act as a disincentive for people who use drugs to attend: 'they will write it all down and the paper will follow you all through your life' (Interview, *Svenska Brukarföreningen* Stockholm Coordinator; Former Drug User). Those in substitution therapy who attend can therefore be reported to their opiate substitution therapy centres, and, with needle and injecting paraphernalia requirement assumed to indicate ongoing or recommencing drug use, this can result in withdrawal of substitution therapy; this clearly serves as a strong disincentive for those who are receiving opiate substitution therapy to acquire sterile drug paraphernalia from the needle and syringe programmes, for fear of losing access to their healthcare provision, thus undermining the needle and syringe programmes ambition of reducing drug-related harm.

'If you have methadone and you want to relapse and you go there, then they phone the clinic, and say *name redacted* was here.'

(Interview, Chair and Founder of *Svenska Brukarföreningen*; Drug User)

'If you have methadone and you went to the [Malmö or Lund] needle exchange, they're going into your journal, and then they see "oh you have methadone", and the methadone clinic gets informed... maybe they finish your methadone.'

(Interview, *Svenska Brukarföreningen* Stockholm Coordinator; Former Drug User)

Swedish needle and syringe programmes are high threshold, with a minimum age of 20 (Månsson et al. 2000), and the Malmö exchange is closed after 3 p.m. and on weekends, exacerbating difficulties in accessing these services. Indeed, needle and syringe programmes have been noted to fail in preventing infection transmission due to stringent regulations resulting in barriers to accessing services

(Des Jarlais et al. 1995; Stimson 1989; also see INPUD 2015). Moreover, respondents noted these needle and syringe programmes provide only needles, and not other injection paraphernalia. This is very concerning, since the sharing of paraphernalia, including cookers and filters, can facilitate hepatitis C transmission (Degenhardt and Hall 2012; Health Protection Agency et al. 2007; Patrick et al. 2001; Rhodes 2002; Rhodes et al. 2004): 'prevention messages aimed at Drug Users must go beyond simply advising against sharing needles and should discourage sharing of any injection equipment'. (Patrick et al. 2001: 892). And so, where 'paraphernalia are presumably also important' (Månsson et al. 2000: 257) in determining hepatitis C transmission even when needle sharing does not occur, hepatitis B and C 'continued to spread at high rates' (Månsson et al. 2000: 253) at the Malmö needle and syringe programme; this has been, per the first below quotation, (mis)interpreted as indicating that the needle and syringe programme has failed to decrease needle sharing, with this argument used to inform anti-harm reduction arguments (espoused by those including the same key respondent quoted below) claiming that these programmes fail to work in reducing the transmission of blood-borne infections; in reality, however, the failures of these services are due to the lack of *comprehensive* and well-realised harm reduction.

> 'You could also see that people are probably sharing needles also in Malmö and Lund. You can see this from the hepatitis. So it's [needle exchange] not a solution to make drug users not using dirty needles.'
>
> (Interview, Senior Advisor – Ministry of Social Affairs)

> 'The needle exchanges in Malmö and Lund, the only two there are in Sweden, they only give you like the pump and the needle. And it's the spoon and the filter and all that shit that gives you the hepatitis C.'
>
> (Interview, RFHL, Drug User)

> 'You have to be the age of twenty, and you have to show them ID, and they only provide syringes and needles. Not sterile water, not alcohol swabs, not the spoon, not the filter, nothing.'
>
> (Interview, Chair and Founder of *Svenska Brukarföreningen*; Drug User)

Outside Malmö and Lund, illegal needle and syringe programmes and/or provision in hospitals have reportedly operated to fill the void in service provision. In addition, *Svenska Brukarföreningen*, the Swedish Drug Users' Union, have operated a free, informal needle and syringe programme in Stockholm, with this organisation of people who use drugs forced to fill the considerable gaps in state-sponsored service provision.

> 'In many places, I know in Västerås, and in Umeå, in some few places, there were illegal needle exchange [programmes] on [at] the hospitals. Because the personnel didn't accept [the legislation]. They saw the need.'
>
> (Interview, RFHL)

> 'Some doctors in dealing with HIV patients are giving them free needles.'
>
> (Interview, Senior Advisor – Ministry of Social Affairs)

Further to the notable lack of state provision of clean needles and injecting paraphernalia, it is illegal for pharmacies and shops to sell needles and syringes to people who use drugs (EMCDDA 2010). As is discussed in Chapter 6, people who use drugs therefore have to go to dangerous lengths to acquire their needles illegally.

> 'No [you're not allowed to buy needles]. But you're not allowed to buy drugs either.'
>
> (Interview, Psychiatrist working with drug addiction; Previously with RNS)

> 'There's a law that forbids chemists to sell needles and syringes to a drug user. And… I think that's a very important part of the story, because if you could buy it from the chemist, then the absence of needle exchange wouldn't be like, so devastating.'
>
> (Interview, *Svenska Brukarföreningen* Stockholm Coordinator; Former Drug User)

Since in 'Sweden both sales and the carrying of drug injection equipment have been prohibited' (Amundsen 2003: 254), there are reports of the Swedish authorities and police destroying injecting paraphernalia, with reports of 'policemen wrecking, tearing the needles apart, or taking the needles away from drug users, in Stockholm' (Interview, Social Worker, Malmö Prostitution Unit). These legally sanctioned, state-sponsored efforts serve to exacerbate the harms which can be associated with drug use, notably blood-borne infections and risks of violence (Deering et al. 2014). As such, these interventions actively increase the difficulties faced by people who use drugs to use their drugs hygienically and safely; such efforts are driven by, at the very least, a simple indifference to the wellbeing of people who use drugs and to the harms that may be associated with drug use.

Education

Safer drug use

Provision of information concerning how to use drugs more safely is heavily problematised in Sweden, seen, like needle and syringe provision, as facilitating and endorsing criminalised activity. Education instead is limited to 'just say no' messages and scare campaigns discouraging the use of drugs:

> 'we give them [young people] information about the drugs being dangerous, and that's why they are illegal… so they should just keep away… Not anything else. Not use a little, or use once a week or anything. They just should not use. That's the message.'
>
> (Interview, IOGT-NTO; Previously RNS)

> 'If a drug user comes [to a hospital] to ask "how do I inject without causing harm to myself?" they won't tell you, because that's the same as kind of aid, they won't aid you.'
>
> (Interview, RFHL, Drug User)

Swedish schools have a long tradition of drugs, alcohol, and tobacco education (EMCDDA 2008), but its empiricism and effectiveness is questionable: patronising slogans designed to discourage and frighten children off trying drugs, such as '*knark är bajs*' ('drugs are poo') crudely conflate and over-simplify the relative harms of different drugs.

> 'Our type of harm reduction is to try to convince people that drugs are bad. And do everything that is in our power to convince them, and one way of convincing them is to have a tough legislation.'
>
> (Interview, Stockholm Police [Narcotics Division Team Leader])

> 'They had one some years ago that was called "*knark är bajs*", you know, "drugs is poo", I mean, who takes that seriously?'
>
> (Interview, RFHL, Drug User)

Responsibility for acquiring and providing information on how to reduce harm is seen to be that of people who use drugs, who are expected either to learn from one another, to educate themselves (online, for example), or to learn from experiencing difficulty and harm personally. This is in stark contrast to harm reduction education initiatives in other countries, with the UK government and National Health Service, for example, running clinics and drop-ins, as well as websites and helplines, to discuss and/or provide information pertaining to specific drug-related harms, harm reduction, safer drug using information, injecting drug use, club drug use, and so forth, in stark juxtaposition to Sweden's policies.

> 'I think they can teach each other. I mean, the drug users, they are very good at doing what they're doing, and they're very good at also giving help, you know, rescue people with overdoses. If one is alive, they will both survive.'
>
> (Interview, Psychiatrist working with drug addiction; Previously with RNS)

Information on blood-borne infections

In addition to opposition to various harm reduction interventions, there is very limited availability of information surrounding blood-borne infections that are important for communities of people who use and inject drugs. Sweden's two needle and syringe programmes are noted to provide such information (Ljungberg 1991), but this is by no means the norm, especially when it comes to hepatitis C, the most important blood-borne infection impacting people who inject drugs globally (Health Protection Agency et al. 2007), and, as is discussed further in Chapter 6, a considerable problem amongst people who inject drugs in Sweden.

> 'No one has ever offered me a test. And that's also kind of strange, because of that law that says that this is a real serious disease and you can lock people up if they like don't protect others from getting it... There's a lot of situations when they could tell me that "look, hepatitis C exists..." [T]his is a disease that people relate to drug users, and the awareness of... the seriousness isn't there.'
>
> (Interview, *Svenska Brukarföreningen* Stockholm Coordinator; Former Drug User)

> 'We don't even get any information about things like hepatitis C and things like that. I didn't even know what it was before I had it.'
>
> (Interview, RFHL, Drug User)

Opiate substitution therapy

Opposition to substitution therapy

Opiate substitution therapy – that is, the provision of buprenorphine and methadone for people who have opiate dependencies – remains controversial in many contexts both in Sweden and in other states. Further to concerns that harm reduction in general may encourage or endorse drug use, there is a fear in some states that these policies will be a 'slippery slope' towards liberalisation of drug control laws, and will ultimately result in drug legalisation. A blanket condemnation of 'drugs' has resulted in opiate substitution programmes – such as methadone or buprenorphine substitution for heroin and opiate dependency – being seen to be problematic (Drucker et al. 1998), perceived as 'simply substituting one drug for another' (Des Jarlais 1995: 1580), and thus essentially seen to endorse drug use, irrespective of positive results of these programmes in reducing the incidence of blood-borne infections and improving the quality of life of those with opiate dependency, and in spite of these drugs being classed by the World Health Organization as *essential medicines* (WHO 2015).[8]

Despite such opposition to opiate substitution, Sweden was one of the first European states to adopt methadone substitution therapy (Anker 2007; UNODC 2006). Though Sweden may therefore be seen as something of a trailblazer, substitution therapy is seen by some key stakeholders in Sweden, along the lines of abovementioned international concerns, to involve simply replacing one detrimental narcotic with another, counterproductive to achieving Sweden's goal of a drug-free society (Van der Giessen and Van Brussel 1996). Social constructions of people who use drugs and of those pathologised as drug 'addicts' continue here, with methadone and opiate substitution therapies seen to perpetuate the lack of ability of people who use drugs to engage, in a normatively acceptable sense, with (Swedish) reality:

> 'They're still walking around in a big fog, and they don't know what's happening around them.'
>
> (Interview, KRIS)

'Methadone and Subutex, they won't make you cured, if you understand what I mean, you're still addicted to another type of drugs, but that's legal.'

(ibid.)

'In general opinion I am like a drug zombie. I don't think I am. I don't think anyone could, if they meet me, could detect.'

(Interview, *Svenska Brukarföreningen* Stockholm Coordinator; P-Drug User)

'We have the idea of drug-free society. Then it should be little bit difficult to come into substitution therapy, if that could be seen as an easy way out.'

(Interview, Senior Advisor – Ministry of Social Affairs)

There is further concern in Sweden that opiate substitution therapy will result in high levels of 'leakage' into the illicit market, again undermining Sweden's prohibitionist ambitions. With drug use itself constructed as a disease in Sweden (discussed in Chapter 2), spreading from person to person, substitution therapy is seen to facilitate the continued spread of this epidemic.

'It went catastrophic: the legally prescribed drugs was spread from the drug addicts out to young kids… it was like epidemic spreading of drugs, because they could go to a pharmacy and pick out drugs for free, and they gave to their friends, and their friends gave to other friends, so it started to spread.'

(Interview, Stockholm Police [Narcotics Division Team Leader])

'A lot of them [people who use drugs], when they are getting the benefit of being [getting] help from the society, at first they are very thankful, and they take this very serious, but a lot of them are going back to their old habits, and their old patterns, and starting to use, misuse the fact that the government supplies them with methadone, so we have a lot of people, they are getting legally prescribed methadone from different clinics and things like that, and they go down with their legally prescribed drugs, go down to *Plattan* [Stockholm's famous drug scene] and sell.'

(Interview, Stockholm Police [Narcotics Division Team Leader])

'They think that we always are lying and trying to get methadone or something, you know, to get drugs somehow, cheating.'

(Interview, *Svenska Brukarföreningen*; Former Drug User)

And though opiate substitution is available for people who use drugs in Sweden, inadequate training of social service and healthcare providers, coupled with stigmatisation of people who use drugs (itself informed by prohibitionist discourse and conflations of drugs and opiates), can result in a reluctance on the part of service and healthcare providers to provide services and opiate substitution to people who use drugs, even when it is legally permitted and required.

> 'When doctors say "no, I can't help you, because it's illegal to do drugs". It happens... "I can't proscribe methadone or buprenorphine for you, because it's illegal, and we have [a] drug-free society as a goal and methadone is a drug..." I know doctors as well who wants to help people, but they don't dare... Because of the attitudes again, they so scared to be attacked... "you're a drug dealing doctor".'
>
> (Interview, Chair and Founder of *Svenska Brukarföreningen*; Drug User)

Substitution therapy availability

As of 2007, there were 3,115 individuals reported to be in opiate substitution therapy in Sweden, on methadone or on buprenorphine (Subutex) (EMCDDA 2010). Between 2003 and 2007, numbers in substitution therapy increased by more than 40% (EMCDDA 2009). However, as with needle and syringe programmes in Sweden, there are regional disparities in substitution therapy availability, predominantly available in major cities (Lindberg and Haynes 2000). Depending on location, respondents noted varying waiting times for substitution therapy, and a complete lack of availability in some parts of the country. These variations in healthcare provision are again allowed for by municipal independence.

> 'Some parts of [the] country, they say "no we don't like this programme. We won't have this here."'
>
> (Interview, RFHL)

> '... methadone and buprenorphine treatment, now it begins to be accepted in Stockholm, and Malmö. But not in Gothenburg... and not either in small places... they don't even offer that treatment, because they say there's no need.'
>
> (Interview, RFHL)

> 'You live in Stockholm, then you get methadone or buprenorphine like in three months, at least three months after you asked for it, you get it. If you're living in Skåne, in the south of Sweden, it's a year.'
>
> (Interview, *Svenska Brukarföreningen* Stockholm Coordinator; Former Drug User)

Difficulties and experiences of people who use drugs in gaining and maintaining access to substitution programmes are discussed in the following chapters.

The Malmö model – a second 'Swedish model'?

I have stressed elsewhere (Levy 2015) that a notable deviation from normative Swedish understandings and discourse is what may be referred to as the 'Malmö model' of service provision, which focusses on harm reduction, not only for people who use drugs through their needle and syringe programmes, but additionally for sex workers through the state-sponsored Malmö Prostitution Unit. This has been conspicuous by its divergence from Swedish dominant discourse and policy, something of an outlier from the remainder of the *folkhemmet*. As I have stressed (Levy 2015), this is despite considerable opposition to harm reduction espoused by key stakeholders and politicians elsewhere in the country:

> 'It's minimising the risk so when the time comes that if you maybe wanna stop doing what you're doing, you're as whole as you can be.'
>
> (Interview, Social Worker, Malmö Prostitution Unit; also quoted in Levy 2015)

> '... needle exchange, it is just the same as condoms for sex workers... If you're a sex worker, to avoid diseases, you need the condoms. If you're a drug user, to avoid diseases, you need clean syringes and clean needles.'
>
> (Interview, *Svenska Brukarföreningen* Stockholm Coordinator; Former Drug User; also quoted in Levy 2015)

> 'From a pragmatic point of view, that you do whatever's necessary for, the main thing is to help people, to save lives.'
>
> (Interview, RFHL, Drug User; also quoted in Levy 2015)

Thus, a notion of a cohesive Swedish prohibitionist positioning in opposition to harm reduction interventions for people who use drugs (and other communities) is called into question by the situation in the south of Sweden.

> 'Like needle exchange. We had it for twenty years [in Malmö]... we so far apart from each other. And you can see it in this topic too. You can see it prostitution.'
>
> (Interview, Social Worker, Malmö Prostitution Unit; also quoted in Levy 2015)

> '[It] is a little bit different between the different parts in Sweden, you know, like in Malmö. They work more focussed on harm reduction.'
>
> (Interview, National Coordinator Against Trafficking and Prostitution; also quoted in Levy 2015)

As I have stressed elsewhere, this should be seen to be due to the fact that Malmö is considerably distant from the Swedish capital, and easily accessible to continental Europe (see Figure 4.1) and to what may be seen to be a more pragmatic (vis-à-vis drugs policy) Copenhagen, Denmark (Anker 2007), now linked to Malmö via the 2010 Öresund Bridge.

> 'The closeness to Denmark. Really, it matters. It matters. In both issues [drug use and sex work policy/discourse]... the scientists that work in Malmö, for

instance, they say that as well. They say “well, you know, the further you are from the capital, the more free you are to think and to act”.’

(Interview, Chair of RFHL; also quoted in Levy 2015)

‘If you look at it geographically, both Stockholm and Gothenburg are very isolated, as cities. Malmö has… Copenhagen… I mean, you have the government there [in Stockholm].’

(Interview, Social Worker, Malmö Prostitution Unit; also quoted in Levy 2015)

‘Skåne [southern province containing Malmö and Lund] always sticks out. The people from there, the politicians and the general attitude there is more continental.’

(Interview, RNS; also quoted in Levy 2015)

‘The renaissance kind of stopped at Copenhagen, it didn’t get through the forests in Småland [province bordering Skåne to the north], we didn’t get it to Stockholm.’

(Interview, RFHL; also quoted in Levy 2015)

‘The Southern part of Sweden is very close to Denmark. They tend to share the same ideas, be more what they call “liberal”… and they are more influenced, I think, from other countries.’

(Interview, Police [National Rapporteur for Prostitution and Trafficking]; also quoted in Levy 2015)

‘They are culturally closer also, to the Danes. Yeah. More liberal I think.’

(Interview, Gender Consultant; Previously *Kvinnoforum*; also quoted in Levy 2015)

Summary: variability of services and harm exacerbation

‘All groups, all citizens, must be given the highest standard of health service, and they can’t deny you healthcare out of ideology or moral. Healthcare must be given to everyone out of science and research. But in Sweden, some groups are denied… Instead of harm reduction, this is harm maximisation.’

(Interview, Chair and Founder of *Svenska Brukarföreningen* [also quoted in Levy 2015: 153])

Evidence-based assistance, treatment, and/or intervention for people who use drugs, specifically harm reduction programmes and services, are frequently sidelined in many states in favour of punishment and incarceration (Drucker et al. 1998; Global Commission on Drug Policy 2011). This is certainly the case in Sweden, a state that has remained staunchly opposed to evidence-based harm reduction

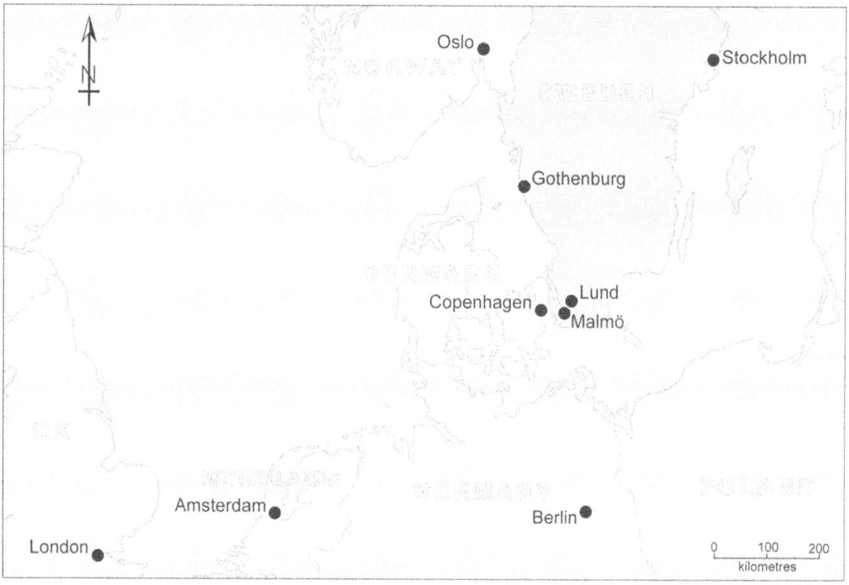

Figure 4.1 Map showing Sweden's relative position in Europe. Note Malmö's proximity to Denmark, and Stockholm's relative isolation.

interventions, despite its reputation as an advanced, 'liberal' welfare state. Progress has been slow in implementation of harm reduction, and the only well-established needle and syringe programmes in Sweden have failed to provide comprehensive harm reduction interventions, only providing what may be regarded as fairly limited services. Harm reduction is understood in Sweden to encourage and endorse drug use, and so is seen by many stakeholders to be incompatible with Sweden's aim to achieve a 'drug-free society'. Instead of provision of harm reduction services, the preferred Swedish state-sponsored projects are what I term 'harm exacerbation' (also see Levy 2015), or what the above-quoted respondent refers to as 'harm maximisation'. Harms that may result from drug use – whether as a result of the drug use itself, or as an indirect result of criminalisation, stigma, and social exclusion – are seen to encourage individuals to cease their drug use, and are therefore seen to be acceptable means to Sweden's prohibitionist ends. Additionally, the type and extent of service provision for people who use drugs are inconsistent across the country: municipal independence allows for variability of which services are available and how they are realised. It has allowed for what may be regarded as progress towards an adoption of pragmatic services in some areas of Sweden's People's Home, and stubborn hostility and resistance to them in others.

Having focussed in this chapter on how Swedish discourse has impacted what services are available for people who use drugs in Sweden, in the next chapter I explore the experiences of people who use drugs of Swedish service and healthcare provision.

Notes

1 It is important to stress that not all of the outcomes of drug use are necessarily harmful. Though I list drug dependence in the main body of the text as something which can be harmful or can have adverse outcomes surrounding it, I must emphasise that whether an individual's drug dependence comes to be problematic for that individual is subjective, nuanced, and complex. I am at pains to emphasise that drug dependence should not, by default, be assumed and/or moralised to be problematic or harmful.

2 It should be noted that there are considerable discrepancies between the UNODC 2011 and 2014 figures vis-à-vis HIV prevalence amongst people who inject drugs (13.1% HIV prevalence is estimated in the 2014 report). As stressed by Harm Reduction International (HRI) and the International Network of People who Use Drugs (INPUD 2014b), such discrepancy does not necessarily indicate a substantial change in actual prevalence, but could well have more to do with varying methodological approaches in data gathering.

3 To reiterate, figures are estimates at best – other estimates place this figure of people who inject drugs with hepatitis C at 10 million (Global Commission on Drug Policy 2013); a review of available literature suggests between 60% and 80% of people who inject drugs are living with hepatitis C (Nelson et al. 2011).

4 The WHO, UNODC, UNAIDS specify nine pillars of harm reduction with a heavy focus on HIV and blood-borne infection transmission. The harm reduction interventions listed in my prose, however, include interventions to reduce a broader set of drug-related harms. The nine pillars are:

> 1. Needle and syringe programmes (NSPs) 2. Opioid substitution therapy (OST) and other drug dependence treatment 3. HIV testing and counselling (T&C) 4. Antiretroviral therapy (ART) 5. Prevention and treatment of sexually transmitted infections (STIs) 6. Condom programmes for IDUs and their sexual partners 7. Targeted information, education and communication (IEC) for IDUs and their sexual partners 8. Vaccination, diagnosis and treatment of viral hepatitis 9. Prevention, diagnosis and treatment of tuberculosis.
>
> (WHO, UNODC, UNAIDS 2009: 6)

Community distribution of naloxone was added to a subsequent rewrite.

5 Opposition to harm reduction has been directed towards other groups too, with examples including opposition to condoms and dental dams in prisons (Yap et al. 2007), tied in with an intolerance of same-sex sexual practice (Dolan et al. 1995), and problematisation of harm reduction initiatives for sex workers (for arguments in opposition to sex work-related harm reduction, see Farley 2004; Raymond 2004; for analysis of opposition to sex work-related harm reduction, see Brooks-Gordon 2006; Levy 2011; Levy 2015; Weitzer 2008).

6 HIV and hepatitis C testing and counselling are also put forward as preferential alternatives by some notable Swedish opponents of harm reduction and needle and syringe programmes, as they are not seen to facilitate or encourage drug use as needle and syringe programmes are (see Amundsen et al. 2003; Käll et al. 2007), and it is argued that the implementation of these programmes will result in a peripheralisation of such preferable initiatives (testing and counselling). This is in spite of the fact that it is argued that needle and syringe programmes should operate within a larger infrastructure and context of service provision (Advisory Council on the Misuse of Drugs 2009; Darke and Hall 2003), not in isolation or as replacement initiatives for existing measures. In short, needle and syringe programmes are emphasised to be most effective when they *include* services such as testing and counselling. To argue that these programmes divert attention or resources from such services, that these interventions are alternatives that one has to choose between, is arguably deliberately misleading.

7 It may be stressed additionally that focussing on *levels* of drug use serves to eclipse a focus on reducing the potential harms of drug use – whether these stem from the drug use in and of itself, or whether driven by prohibition and criminalisation.

8 Along these lines, in the UK Home Office's 2012 outline of drugs strategy there is specific opposition to substitution treatment, constructed as 'replacement of one dependency with another' (Home Office 2012: 10). This is an apparent opposition to dependency *per se*, irrespective of the report conceding that some on opiate substitution 'have jobs, positive family lives and are no longer taking illegal drugs or committing crime'. The title of the report – '*Putting Recovery First*' – is clear, as is the above quotation regarding opiate substitution therapy: however unproblematic, successful, and stable the life of a drug user may be, the point is that their drug use renders them normatively inferior to a drug/dependence-free equivalent.

5 Experiences of service and healthcare provision

> 'We are humans and have the same worth, I think, so we should be treated in the same way.'
>
> (Interview, Former Sex Worker; Former Drug User)

Having focussed on which services are available for people who use drugs in Sweden, specifically Sweden's opposition to harm reduction interventions, in this chapter I now focus on the experiences of people who use drugs in accessing service and healthcare provision in Sweden. Conditionality of service provision, as well as disciplining and control from service providers, will be areas of specific focus of this chapter.

Social exclusion and marginalisation have broad impacts on health for people who use drugs (WHO 2004), with Des Jarlais et al. (1995) stressing that people who use drugs need to be treated as individuals, not according to stereotypes and clichés by healthcare and service providers. However, in Sweden, legislation and pathologising, infantilising, and generalising discourses surrounding drugs, the people who use them, and drug use have detrimentally fed through into the attitudes and policies of Swedish service providers. Criminalisation and stigmatisation have resulted in an extensive denial of the services and healthcare that are provided for, and are accessible to, 'normative' Swedes.

> 'Ask anyone. They [drug users] don't get the same kind of treatment… they don't have full citizenship actually, as they are refused help in many different ways and in many different places.'
>
> (Interview, Chair of RFHL)

> 'Sweden should be… following these human rights and everything, but that doesn't include drug users.'
>
> (Interview, Former Sex Worker; Former Drug User)

> 'Most fundamental human rights are not your rights anymore.'
>
> (Interview, RFHL)

Spatial segregation

As individuals who have consumed drugs are criminalised, tolerance of the presence of people who use drugs in public areas becomes problematic, implying an endorsing of criminal activity, with totalising social construction, as well as criminalisation, serving to reduce individuals to nothing but their drug use and, therefore, their default criminality. Police policy of displacing people who use drugs and drug scenes, discussed in Chapter 3, is thus augmented by effective expulsion from civil society.

> 'In Sweden… you don't want to deal with drug users anywhere, and if you complain about it, it's always said that "It's illegal to use drugs. You're a criminal, just get lost."'
>
> (Interview, RFHL, Drug User)

> 'Most of the problems here in Sweden connect to the criminalisation. I mean, the mentality behind the professionals, I mean, it's illegal to do drugs.'
>
> (Interview, Chair and Founder of *Svenska Brukarföreningen*; Drug User)

> '[Drug Users are] [e]xtremely marginalised… because if you are reduced, as a person, to be nothing but a drug addict, I mean if you're looking for help because you have a bad knee, and you get the answer "you're a drug user", "yeah, I know, but I have a bad knee". "Well you're a drug user." You are reduced to this one and only thing. You are a drug user. You are not anymore a father or a son or a sister or a brother.'
>
> (Interview, Chair of RFHL)

During my fieldwork, numerous instances were cited of people who use drugs being asked to leave pharmacies, doctors' surgeries, and public areas, reducing their access to healthcare and service provision, with this seemingly driven by a 'belief that drug users cannot be trusted to use health services appropriately' (Des Jarlais et al. 1995: 1579). Respondents additionally reported that they had encountered pejorative language and discriminatory treatment from healthcare providers, again serving as barriers to accessing services and acting as disincentive to seek services.

> 'If I'm at the hospital and want healthcare, if I'm a drug user, it's perfectly okay to just kick me out. It's perfectly okay to deny me, you know, at social services, money to [for] food or somewhere to stay or anything, clothes, anything, it's perfectly alright, because it's illegal to use drugs.'
>
> (Interview, RFHL, Drug User)

> 'They look more down on you… [you] have these scars [from injecting], maybe bad teeth, and like that and stuff, but if you are like a sweet little girl

they say "Oh, poor you"... I heard a lot of my friends, especially male friends, that they have been, like the healthcare staff have been really rude to them.'

(Interview, Former Sex Worker; Former Drug User)

'I had an old boyfriend, he was buying amphetamine, and he take a shot of that, and it was not like amphetamine... he was so afraid, and soon he couldn't walk and he called for an ambulance, and then at the hospital they said, he heard the nurses speaking to each other, and they said "Oh, it was not so bad, he has himself to blame if he get poisoned".'

(ibid.)

One drug user respondent was asked to leave a pharmacy when his status as a drug user was disclosed, and had also been forcibly removed from a doctor's appointment when the doctor saw physical signs of injecting drug use. He returned after his drug use had ceased, and was then given the surgery his ailment necessitated:

'I went to the pharmacy to get some information about methadone, and they were very polite, and I said, when I said "I'm in methadone treatment myself..." her attitude changed, and she just said 'No, that's, you have to go somewhere else". She just shut off her computer, and asked me to leave.'

(Interview, RFHL, Drug User)

'I went to hospital to get help with... my hip... then he [the doctor] saw the puncture marks on my arm and... he called for two guards that came and threw me out. And he said "This is a drug addict, he's probably just here to try go get some pills and stuff." And they threw me out... when I was out of treatment and clean and sober, I got the operation at the same place that they threw me out some years earlier. So when you're on drugs, you don't get medical care, you're treated like shit.'

(ibid.)

In addition to assumptive concern that people who use drugs will attempt to acquire medication illegitimately, it is assumed that people who use drugs will steal needles and paraphernalia for drug use if they are given access to spaces of healthcare provision; this is something of a tautologous assumption, since drug users having to illicitly acquire injecting paraphernalia may be argued to be due to the failure of those very same service and healthcare providers to provide people who use drugs with harm reduction services and tools to use drugs safely. In short: healthcare providers refuse to provide people who use drugs with the sterile needles and syringes they require for their health and wellbeing; healthcare providers blame people who use drugs for attempting to steal the needles and syringes.

'They [drug users] usually make a lot of trouble when they go into the ordinary healthcare system... the wards are not built for drug users, they can

> go, they can sneak into the nurses rooms and steal needles… so they're not really welcome in the ordinary health system.'
>
> (Interview, Psychiatrist working with drug addiction; Previously with RNS)

Further to assumptions that people who use drugs will act in a disorderly manner in spaces involved in the provision of healthcare, they are effectively viewed as a lost and undeserving cause for healthcare provision. Since people who use drugs are seen as disrupting and impeding Sweden's aspiration to achieve a clean and ordered *folkhemmet*, they are essentially seen as a waste of resources that could be allocated to non-deviant citizens:

> '"[It is thought that] If I cure you, you'll probably die, and I'll have done this for nothing. You're trying to kill yourself anyway, so why should I help you? What do you need teeth for? You don't eat anyway." Where you get kind of excluded from the human rights, you don't [get] looked upon and treated like a human being. You [are] treated worse than a dog.'
>
> (Interview, RFHL, Drug User)

People who use drugs thus experience segregation and displacement from public and institutional space, and those in treatment for dependence can also experience segregation from normative healthcare, for example with methadone clinics separated from mainstream healthcare provision. Such compartmentalisation of medical services not only implies a distinction between certain Swedish citizens, but additionally exacerbates stigma. One respondent (Interview, Former Drug User) avoided going to collect her Subutex when her children were home sick 'because I don't want to take my children with me to this place'. We see, then, how such siloing of services results in significant barriers to health, in people being unable to access said services.

> 'We [do] not allow general practitioners to [prescribe] those substitution therapies, you have to be in a treatment.'
>
> (Interview, Senior Advisor – Ministry of Social Affairs)

> 'Substitution therapy should be in the primary care, I mean, all these special clinics, it's rubbish.'
>
> (Interview, Chair and Founder of *Svenska Brukarföreningen*; Drug User)

> 'I think there is lots of idiotic rules, I think that it would be possible to give me methadone in the same way as I get other treatments from hospitals, just a contact between me and a doctor.'
>
> (Interview, *Svenska Brukarföreningen* Stockholm Coordinator; Former Drug User)

> 'As patients we should just be another group in the healthcare. And the same rules that goes for other groups should go for us as well. That is not the case.'
>
> (ibid.)

Constructions of people who use drugs as untrustworthy and dangerous have informed these medical compartmentalisations, where, as noted above, people who use drugs are 'not really welcome in the ordinary health system' (Interview, Psychiatrist working with drug addiction; Previously with RNS). Concern about the apparent violence and criminality of people who use drugs indeed results in some methadone centres erecting signs which I saw during fieldwork, signs stressing that bringing weapons into centres may result in methadone withdrawal. One such sign from a Stockholm methadone centre read: 'Carrying all forms of weapons is prohibited. If it comes to our attention that you have weapons we will make a police report and report you to the kick out group [group deciding whether to withdraw methadone access]. [My translation]' Similarly, the Malmö needle and syringe programme displayed signs to discourage break-in attempts, with the sign in the Malmö needle and syringe programme window reading: 'The needle exchange is empty on evenings, nights, and weekends. There isn't anything to steal! [My translation]' Such break-ins further highlight the difficulty of obtaining sterile needles and syringes, not to mention the barriers presented by heavily restricted opening hours, all of which have led to the desperation of people who need to break into a service provision centre in order to get the needles that they need. The difference between healthcare provision for normative and deviant society seems clear from these signs, with an assumption that people who use drugs, criminal by default, are unsafe and disruptive.

> 'That's [the sign in the methadone centre] just because you are a methadone patient. This will not, we won't see this in any other kind of healthcare treatment… you're treated like you're a criminal, you're potentially a criminal. And you're potentially violent, you're a liar, you never tell the truth, you're manipulative, and all this, we meet that all day.'
>
> (Interview, RFHL, Drug User)

Social services

The engagement of Swedish social services with people who use drugs (and other marginalised communities [Levy 2015]) is frequently informed by mainstream dominant discourse and social construction, resulting in conditional assistance and judgemental and unhelpful responses from these service providers.

> 'In other countries it's a lifesaving thing. You know, you do very pragmatic, where you focus on saving lives and curing people. Here you have the focus on control and on punishment.'
>
> (Interview, RFHL, Drug User)

Swedish social services 'have a tremendous amount of power' (Interview, RFHL; also see Hallam 2010) vis-à-vis their clients' treatment and access to services. Social services become involved with people who use drugs seeking state-sponsored assistance from the outset, even where the case requires medical intervention or treatment; the majority of treatment is therefore organised outside of hospitals and the medical sphere (EMCDDA 2010).

> 'To get into detox, you have to have the social service behind you. You have to go to them. Which is very weird... you can be almost dying, but... a social worker has to sign the paper.'
>
> (Interview, RFHL, Drug User)

Demonisation and infantilisation of people who use drugs informs how some social workers engage with their clients, respondents noting patronising and belittling interactions driven by assumptions of people who use drugs as criminal, unreliable, dangerous, manipulative, and pathological.

> 'Even people in the social programme at the university were taught that people with drug problems were, by definition, manipulative.'
>
> (Interview, RFHL)

> '[It is thought that] if you are a drug user in Sweden, you can't be trusted. You always got a hidden agenda... And if the one that you are supposed to have a contact with has that picture of you, then the contact gets a little bit difficult.'
>
> (Interview, *Svenska Brukarföreningen* Stockholm Coordinator; Former Drug User)

> 'With social services it's like, it's very much like when you're a drug addict... you're almost treated like a child.'
>
> (Interview, RFHL, Drug User)

Seeking help with drug-related problems can result in invasions of privacy and domestic harassment by the social services. One respondent's wife, a childminder, was confronted by social services in her home, who threatened to inform the parents of the children she looked after that she had the respondent, a drug user, living with her, in spite of the fact that she no longer resided with him. The confrontation resulted in her losing her job. Another respondent, (also quoted below), was harassed at home by social services who attempted to search her property and question her husband following her enrolment in substitution therapy. She was then told that she had to attend a specific clinic to give birth or she would lose her buprenorphine access, using the threat of withdrawal of healthcare provision as a means to essentially blackmail compliance, and again enforcing a segregation of people who use drugs within the healthcare sector. Her doctor felt that the stillbirth she subsequently had was due to these stresses to which she had been subjected:

> 'They [social services] said "tomorrow we will call all the kids' parents, and tell them that you have an intravenous drug addict living at home". And at that time, I wasn't even living there… And she's never touched drugs. She doesn't even smoke cigarettes. And she was the one who got punished… they were horrible. There were three of them against my wife. One started screaming and she tried to defend herself, and the second one started and they kind of broke her down.'
>
> (Interview, RFHL, Drug User)

> 'Because I was so stressed, all the time, about if they [social services were] going to come and take the children, or… they say I must go to the other place [antenatal clinic]… the doctor [felt] probably there [it] was the stress. Because I have stress hormones in my body… I think this was because of them I lost my [pregnancy].'
>
> (Interview, Former Drug User)

Opiate substitution therapy

Gaining access

Access to substitution therapy depends on social workers' preferences, in spite of the Swedish Social Services Act (early 1980s) emphasising self-determination and the autonomy of social workers' clients in dictating the direction their care takes (Gould 1989). Opiate substitution therapy can be flatly refused by social workers, in some cases reflecting a preference for drug-free abstinence focussed treatments (also see Anker 2007; Danna 2012), irrespective of the individual's wellbeing and personal predilection. Given little in the way of alternatives, and out of fear of the possibility of compulsory treatment for drug dependence, some people who use drugs requesting opiate substitution therapy may therefore accept other, undesired treatments.

> 'You have to… [experience] failure with drug-free treatment lots of times, before you even can think of getting methadone.'
>
> (Interview, *Svenska Brukarföreningen* Stockholm Coordinator; Former Drug User)

> 'I was so sad and angry over the social service, because they [have] not managed my Subutex [access] too fast, take too long time… because of my social service bitch, I'm sorry, but she forgot to send in the paper to the Subutex clinic.'
>
> (Interview, Former Drug User)

> '"Okay, now you have to go to this twelve step programme", but you already done it five times, and you know it's just a waste of time, a waste of money.

But you agree on it, because otherwise they put the compulsory treatment on you, and lock you up for six months.'

(Interview, Chair and Founder of *Svenska Brukarföreningen*; Drug User)

'That was a condition: "If you want our help" from the social services "it's the twelve step treatment or nothing". It wasn't up to me to decide, which the law says it is.'

(Interview, RFHL, Drug User)

Having had to enter a twelve-step treatment after being refused substitution therapy, the above-quoted respondent became pre-psychotic as a result of his withdrawal. He then relapsed during the treatment, and was physically removed from the treatment centre and left alone at a bus stop in the sparsely populated area of Norrland:

'When I became what's known as pre-psychotic… I was, to be honest, I was scared, I mean shitless, when I was in that psychotic state, you know. So I took something. What could I do?… What did they do, did they, no, they just kicked me out, they put me on a bus stop. I mean, in the middle of fucking Norrland. I didn't even know where I was. "Here's a ticket, here you are", and then they just took off.'

(Interview, RFHL, Drug User)

Respondents reported long and variable waiting times for gaining access to opiate substitution therapy, made all the more difficult by the high-threshold nature of programmes. Proving a long history of opiate use and dependency, which can be required for access to substitution therapy, has also been problematic for some.

'Sometime in the nineties… I wanted to get methadone, to get into treatment, but it was impossible, because I [hadn't] been in any treatment, I hadn't been in jail for any narcotics, you know, I didn't have any documentation.'

(Interview, *Svenska Brukarföreningen*; Former Drug User)

'First you have to prove that you are a drug user, and then you have to prove that you have been a drug user for a certain amount of time. And then it can take up to six months to get into the substitution therapy… You can't be without drugs for six months… it's not human to get those demands. It's like, for me as a normal citizen, if I get sick I go to the doctor.'

(Interview, *Svenska Brukarföreningen*; Ex-Partner of Drug User)

'I applied for methadone, but the social service denied [it], because I was not down the drain enough. So I had to do heroin for another four years.'

(Interview, Chair and Founder of *Svenska Brukarföreningen*; Drug User)

Disciplining and conditionality

> 'They say when you get into methadone treatment, their goal is my... social *utveckling* [development].'
>
> (Interview, RFHL, Drug User)

Conditions are applied to people who use drugs who wish to retain state-sponsored assistance in the form of opiate substitution therapy. Efforts appear to be directed towards disciplining people who use drugs to encourage a societal reintegration and normalisation into the orderly, socially engineered *folkhemmet*, with people who use drugs understood to be disruptive and socially deviant, in need of social conditioning. 'Good' clients may be seen to be those who, in Foucauldian terms, comport themselves *rationally*, with *discipline*, who comply with regulations and conduct themselves 'properly' within substitution therapy spaces (see Ning 2005).

Punctuality, time management, and general good behaviour at centres are key issues, with perceived 'bad' conduct resulting in punishment, expulsion, and withdrawal of access to healthcare and service provision.

> 'When you start your substitution therapy programme, you trust your [social] worker, and as [the] longer you are in the programme, the trust goes down... after two years, you start to see it's not only one problem to have substitution therapy, it's 100 small issues that makes it very hard to cope with.'
>
> (Interview, Chair and Founder of *Svenska Brukarföreningen*; Drug User)

> 'You get the medicine, because you need the medicine, but it is your social behaviour that puts you out of the programme... it's a moral thing more than anything else, that if you don't behave you are thrown out.'
>
> (Interview, Chair of RFHL)

People who use drugs losing access to substitution therapy is a significant problem: most people visit the Swedish Drug Users' Union for sterile needles, but the second largest group are those who require assistance as a result of having been expelled from methadone programmes.

Methadone must be collected from Swedish centres at specified times, with little in the way of the clients' personal obligations taken into account. Respondents described how tardiness can result in half of the prescribed dose being punitively poured away, along with a disciplinary rebuke. Where one respondent was forced by clinic staff to wait until he was late for his appointment, the subsequent reducing of his methadone dosage seems simply spiteful:

> 'I was in a meeting at school with my son... So I called them [the methadone centre] up and said "I'll be late", and then I was sort of punished for being late. I had to go there and then they say "Oh no, you're late, you have to go away again, come back at 1 o'clock"... They keep me from my family... They make it hard for me to work.'
>
> (Interview, RFHL, Drug User)

> 'When I came back, I pressed the [doorbell]... and he opened up, and I was on my way and then he just yelled "Hey stop! You have to wait!" Just yelling, in a very loud voice, and irritable, you know, kind of tone. And he just slammed the door and I stood there out in the stairs, he didn't even let me in.'
>
> (ibid.)

> 'When I came, they made me sort of wait twenty minutes extra, they poured out, they gave me only half the dose of my medication.'
>
> (ibid.)

Though social (re)integration of people who use drugs can be a goal of some harm reduction strategies (Tammi and Hurme 2006), such a focus on time-keeping can ironically be disruptive socially and domestically, and may come to undermine efforts of individuals to keep regular working hours. Where people who use drugs must attend methadone centres within certain time windows, they may therefore have to 'come out' to their employers as being in substitution therapy in order to explain absenteeism and a need to take time off, jeopardising relationships at work and leading to stigma and discrimination from employers and colleagues.

> 'It should have been so easy, if I could just come there once a day *after* work, and get a dose for the next morning, but that's impossible... they are not flexible at all... they don't want to help me until I get, I lose my job, I lose my apartment, maybe in that moment I could get help, I don't know, that's insane.'
>
> (Interview, Former Sex Worker; Former Drug User)

> 'The first six months, when you get into the programme, you have to go to the clinic every morning between half past seven and half past ten, every morning, seven days a week. And if you are employed and you don't want to tell your employer.'
>
> (Interview, *Svenska Brukarföreningen* Stockholm Coordinator; Former Drug User)

> 'If I didn't work here [RFHL], if I had another work... they'd kick me out, I mean they wouldn't accept me going there two or three times a day just in order to piss in a mug, or get my methadone at times that's suitable for them [the clinic], not for me. I mean it's totally hopeless to get any sort of social life as long as you have these bastards hanging over you.'
>
> (Interview, RFHL, Drug User)

As described by the respondent above, people in methadone treatment are subject to urine screening to determine whether they have started using drugs again and/or whether there has been 'leakage' of drugs from the programme (Anker 2007). With methadone provision conditional upon urine samples, abstinence from *all* illicit substance can be required, not only abstinence from drugs that may increase the risk of overdose when used in combination with the opiate substitution therapy, such as opiates, alcohol, benzodiazepines, and tricyclic antidepressants that may medically interact and interfere with some substitution therapy (Darke and Hall 2003). Reductionist discourse, conflating all drug use whilst constructing people who use drugs as certain 'types' of people, is thus seemingly extrapolated into an idea that the use of *any* drug whilst in substitution therapy is a form of relapse into the pathologised behaviours of 'addiction'.

> 'I think methadone treatment [is acceptable], with a lot of restrictions of course... Like, like we have here in Sweden. That they have to prove that they don't use other drugs.'
>
> (Interview, IOGT-NTO; Previously RNS)

> 'I think that's really odd, because the people who's getting in the methadone programme in Sweden, it's people who have the hardest drug problem, who really have tried anything... but in a lot of programme[s] in Sweden, if they just once find out that you have taken anything else, then you are out of the programme immediately.'
>
> (Interview, Politician – The Left Party; Former Drug User)

State-sponsored assistance and services for people who use drugs can therefore be conditional upon the individual becoming entirely free of all drug use, the threat of withdrawal of services intended to catalyse behavioural modification. Other activities that, in some instances, must cease as a condition for substitution therapy were noted by respondents to include gambling and selling sex, apparently characterised as other forms of 'addiction', as incompatible with 'good' behaviour in the People's Home. These services should thus be seen as institutions used as means with which to civilise deviant citizens, remoulding them into normatively acceptable residents of Sweden's *folkhemmet.*

> 'There're people... they will have to sign a contract where they say that they can't continue selling sex, if they continue selling sex they will lose their methadone... some of these people consider selling sex as a form of addiction. So it's like one addiction feeds into the other.'
>
> (Interview, Founder of Swedish sex worker rights organisation, Rose Alliance; Sex Worker)

Simply attempting to negotiate flexible times or experiencing difficulties in passing urine is assumed by some service providers to be indicative of an attempted concealment of continued drug use. Additionally, where staff at methadone centres may *believe* the explanations for the problems in leaving urine, an apparent apathy concerning the welfare and preference of the individual in question may not actually result in any positive action being taken to accommodate said problems. As with the inflexibly specified times of attendance to collect medication, such obstinate rigidity in the collection of urine samples detrimentally impacts the personal and working lives of people who use drugs, a far cry from comprehensively reducing the harms that can be associated with drug use and again erecting barriers in accessing and maintaining access to service and healthcare provision.

> '[My colleague] sometimes has to be [go] to Hungary, sometimes to some other parts of Sweden, and it [leaving regular urine samples] doesn't work for him. And he hasn't show up to give them so many urine samples as they want from him, and he tried to explain "But my life, my work, you must know I need you people"... But their answer is "But the rules. The rules." The rules are more important than how his life really is. So he got threatened to lose his methadone.'
>
> (Interview, *Svenska Brukarföreningen* Stockholm Coordinator; Former Drug User)

> 'I have a hard time, you know, [to] piss on demand. So, and that's a physical reasons for that, prostate thing. And they don't believe me, they just act like I'm making it up, or trying to manipulate my way past it... they said "If you keep on refusing to leave your urinal samples, you will get", I will be questioned and maybe I will lose my treatment... I said "But you know I have these problems, I really can't leave, I really can't piss on demand." "We know that, we've known that since you've started here." And in the beginning I took that as a guarantee that they were about to help me, when they sort of acknowledged what I'd said. But "Yeah, we know, but we don't give a shit"... That's the message.'
>
> (Interview, RFHL, Drug User)

> 'You have to [leave] urine samples, and you really give up your own life.'
>
> (Interview, Politician – The Left Party; Former Drug User)

In addition to urine screening and a focus on punctuality, decorum, and discipline at methadone clinics are of great importance, and punishments and chastisements can be meted out in response to certain behaviours. But what is regarded to be inappropriate behaviour seems to be fairly arbitrary. One individual, for example, was sent for a disciplinary hearing to his methadone centre's *utskrivningsgruppen* ('kick out group') for having a 'bad attitude' (see below quotation). Again, constructions of people who use drugs, infantilisation in particular, feed into policy and practice, individuals seen to require behavioural adjustment, or '*uppfostran*' (upbringing), as quoted below. Preferences of drug users are undermined and disregarded by seemingly capricious rules and decisions imposed by staff, and there is a strong undercurrent of social workers acting seemingly – I do not feel that it is overstatement to say – sadistically, i.e. deliberately and unnecessarily making some of their clients suffer.

> 'He has always been clean in his piss tests, and has always behaved good and you know, no problems at all, and suddenly he was sent to *utskrivningsgruppen* [the kick out group]… he was sent there for bad attitude, because he didn't say "Hi"… they said, "First you have to go because your attitude's so bad", because he didn't, you know, smile and say "Hi".'
>
> (Interview, RFHL, Drug User)

> 'They're [methadone centre staff are] just kind of *uppfostran* [upbringing/education]… something you do with your child, you teach him to behave, you teach him good manners. They are teaching us good manners.'
>
> (ibid.)

> 'It's the attitudes, it's their routines, it's their lack of understanding of the intention of the programme.'
>
> (Interview, RFHL)

> 'They have so much power, because this [methadone] bottle return, the urine samples, it's all about control.'
>
> (Interview, Chair and Founder of *Svenska Brukarföreningen*; Drug User)

Apparently capricious rules appear to vary not only based upon the preference of social workers, but also regionally. Thus, as with other forms of Swedish service provision, access to substitution therapy, conditions and disciplining, and expulsions from treatment are not uniform across the country.

> 'It's so different in the smaller cities in Sweden: if you relapse once, you can get kicked out. If the doctor thinks you have the wrong friends they can kick you out. But in Stockholm it's no longer a problem. I mean, to get kicked out for relapse in Stockholm, it takes quite a long time.'
>
> (Interview, Chair and Founder of *Svenska Brukarföreningen*; Drug User)

> 'I think it depends very much on in which area in Sweden are you living, what kind of social worker do you have contact with, are [if] you one of the lucky ones that has a nice one.'
>
> (Interview, *Svenska Brukarföreningen* Stockholm Coordinator; Former Drug User)

High threshold substitution therapy: barriers to seeking assistance

> 'That is why I sort of sometimes sort of deliberately come late, because I know it pisses them off. That's the only reason, because I hate them.'
>
> (Interview, RFHL, Drug User)

The above-quoted respondent made a point of protesting his treatment at his methadone centre by being deliberately late to their centres and performing other behavioural resistances. Resistance to the disciplining and punitive approaches in methadone programmes may additionally take less flagrant and more apparently cooperative ('complicit') forms (Ning 2005). However, other respondents felt unable or even fearful to express their dissatisfaction, with individuals concerned about losing rights to treatment and of worsening relationships with staff.

> 'I don't ask for things I know I won't get, and that's some kind of adaptation I don't think I should have to do… there is no problem because I avoid these areas. I like, give up before the fight.'
>
> (Interview, *Svenska Brukarföreningen* Stockholm Coordinator; Former Drug User)

> 'The [methadone] programme in Stockholm was the hardest, the meanest… with a lot of rules and everything, so. And the people who was in the programme, they didn't know what to do because if you was complaining… in public, or try to go to [the] newspaper, they was afraid that then they will get [kicked] out of the programme.'
>
> (Interview, Politician – The Left Party; Former Drug User)

> 'If you kind of go with the system, and accept the way that you are looked upon, talked to, treated, then you're okay.'
>
> (Interview, RFHL, Drug User)

Discipline in methadone centres is part of pervasive authoritative and structural violence and abuse, where accepting conditionality and mistreatment in substitution programmes should be seen in a context of more serious and sometimes physical authoritative abuse and hostility; this is discussed in more detail in the next chapter.

> 'These things [police violence] is why you tend to rather accept the shitty behaviour that you get in, for example, methadone treatment. Because you know that it's no use to sort of make any resistance, because if they can kick my fucking teeth in, and make me pay for it, they can sure as hell pour out some medication.'
>
> (Interview, RFHL, Drug User)

Conditionality, stereotyping, and punitive discipline all act as disincentives for people who use drugs to seek assistance, healthcare, service provision, and help to cease their drug use, should this be desired. Thus Sweden's service provision policies and practices, informed as they are by Swedish prohibitionist discourse, actually ironically undermine prohibitionist ambition to end drug use. As with substitution therapy programmes in other states and contexts, complex regulations surrounding treatment 'all serve to reduce the numbers of heroin addicts who actually receive methadone maintenance' (Des Jarlais et al. 1995: 1580; also see Drucker et al. 1998). As Des Jarlais (1995: 11) also notes, 'it will be important that the legal and regulatory restrictions placed upon them [opiate substitution programmes] do not prevent them from replacing the more harmful products and customs'.

> 'I waited for 27 years before I asked for methadone, because I saw my friends, I saw that the rules were, the standard was set so high that no normal person could live up to it.'
>
> (Interview, *Svenska Brukarföreningen* Stockholm Coordinator; Former Drug User)

Compulsory treatment

Further difficulties are reported in compulsory care for drug dependence. Compulsory treatment is seen to be a necessity in Sweden (despite the fact that it represents a disregard for the agency, self-determination, autonomy, and informed consent of those individuals who end up in such programmes [Stevens 2012]), although the treatment of drug users in compulsory treatment seems not only unsuccessful (Van der Giessen and Van Brussel 1996), but punitive and violent, with abuse and institutionalised violence reported by rights organisation RFHL. Infantilisation of people who use drugs in Sweden appears to allow for degrading and abusive disciplinary treatment not only in substitution programmes and not only in terms of spatial segregation and separation, but additionally in terms of compulsory care, and the compulsory treatment of minors.

> 'You have to do something about it before he [a drug user] dies, you know… And the same thing with young people of course. *But*, how they are treated in those institutions… compared to international conventions, UN's for children and so on, it's [how people are treated in compulsory care in Sweden is] not comparable with what we signed internationally.'
>
> (Interview, RFHL)

> 'They're the kind of laws that doesn't belong in a democracy… compulsory treatment in Sweden is kind of a very degrading form of treating people, you know. You completely powerless… especially compulsory treatment for young people in SIS [*statens institutionsstyrelse* [The National Board of Institutional Care]], where if they disobey they are locked in a room without a toilet and they have to piss and shit on the floor.'
>
> (Interview, RFHL, Drug User)

Again, it should be emphasised that compulsory treatment is applied variably throughout Sweden, with a decentralised medical sphere allowing for inconsistent policy:

> 'So how is it then in Sweden? I mean even with the compulsory treatment, it's so different. I don't hear, it's a very long time [since] I heard about someone [subject to compulsory treatment] in Stockholm.'
>
> (Interview, Chair and Founder of *Svenska Brukarföreningen*)

Disseminating dominant discourse: biopower, geopower, discipline

Sweden continues to embrace projects of modernity, projects that conspicuously involve rationalisation and civilisation of any citizens who are constructed to be deviant and disruptive to Sweden's aspirations to create a clean, ordered, and rational *folkhemmet.* Respondent testimony paints such a picture of Swedish institutions – like Swedish opiate substitution centres: these institutions discipline their clients, attempting to normalise, control, contain, and demarcate their behaviour, and to punish and discipline people who use drugs who are deemed to be deviant, incorrigible, and/or recalcitrant.

These institutions in Sweden should thus be seen as having the purpose of disseminating dominant Swedish discourse as to what is normatively acceptable vis-à-vis behaviour and, indeed, identity (Foucault 1976; also see Dean 1994). As this chapter has shown, conditionality and discipline appear to act as key tools in the arsenal of such institutions.[1] These institutions should be seen along the lines of Foucauldian biopower,[2] with these institutions aiming to regulate and control Swedish citizens (and their bodies), aiming to create docile bodies (Foucault 1979), that is, 'subjected and practised bodies' (Foucault 1979: 138). These are to be transformed and transmuted according to cultural expectations and requirements, oppressive processes of creating normatively acceptable bodies, behaviours, and identities (Foucault 1979; also see Keane 2002; Keane 2009) of reformed (and remorseful) *ex*-drug users[3] (see Keane 2009). Such is the conditionality of Sweden's service and healthcare provision for marginalised communities that those who reject the Swedish state's attempts at reform and reconstruction, face a refusal of admission to the People's Home, an exile from the famous Swedish welfare state. A People's Home… but for which people?

These modernising reconstructions should be seen in the context of Sweden's unique modern history, a history particularly marked by the discourses (and resultant laws and policies) of eugenics, social engineering, state-sponsored repression, and (often violent) social control, as discussed in this book's introduction, and as compared aptly by the below-respondent to the policies, practices, and discourses of the National Socialist fascism of 20th-century Germany (also see Baldwin 2005).

> 'What's happened now, today, is the result of a repressive culture that we have had here since ages. And we weren't very far from how we treated our misbehaving people, I mean compared to how they did in Germany. We were very close to that. We sterilised people by force at large numbers, larger numbers per capita than they did in Germany.'
>
> (Interview, RFHL [also quoted in Levy 2015])

As discussed in Chapter 3, Sweden's projects of modernity and social engineering are not solely confined to the institutional setting, but additionally the broader spatial and civil, where what may be termed *geopower*[4] (in addition to and alongside of biopower) is a key tenet in Sweden's social engineering endeavours.

Geopower may be marked by the use of spatial control, displacement, segregation, and a cleansing, moralising, and policing of public space and civil society.

This is the case also within the institutions that have been the focus of this chapter, marked as they are by spatial segregation, exclusion, and eviction of people who use drugs and/or those who do not conform to expectations of normatively acceptable behaviour. And as with Sweden's projects of discipline, social control, and social (re)construction, biopower and geopower in Sweden are not confined to particular groups and communities but, rather, to the facet(s) of the populace who have come to be represented and imagined as a deviant danger to the homogeneous, safe, ordered Swedish nation state. As with the spatial control that was the focus of Chapter 3, sex workers, as well as drug users are subject to displacement from space, and are *also* subject to the disciplining and conditionality meted out by state-sponsored institutions. As I have explored elsewhere (Levy 2015), Sweden's so-called Prostitution Units – state-funded organisations tasked to decrease levels of prostitution through social work – are marked by exclusions of non-conforming clients, conditionality of services, refusals to provide some services (including some harm reduction interventions), disciplining interactions, and attempts to reform, remould, and rationalise clients; many a parallel, then, with the service provision available (or refused) for people who use drugs.

> 'It's very easy to compare it [treatment of sex workers] with like, you know, treatment for heroin addiction. You know, you will have to be able to comply to these certain rules in order to get your methadone… otherwise we will punish you.'
>
> (Interview, Founder of Rose Alliance; Sex Worker [also quoted in Levy 2015])

Summary: conditionality and discipline

Those services which *are* available for people who use drugs in Sweden – whether they be general healthcare provision, or services targeted specifically towards people who use drugs – are marked by conditionality of service provision, by spatial segregation and social exclusion of people who use drugs from services, by discrimination, by structural violence, and by harassment.

Moreover, these services are used as a means with which to discipline and punish service users who are perceived to be recalcitrant or wayward, used as means with which to normalise and rationalise people who use drugs, who are constructed as pathological, infantile, criminal, and disruptive. Essentially, these institutions that provide services to communities of people who use drugs are used to disseminate dominant Swedish discourse pertaining to drugs, drug use, and people who use drugs; they are used to socially engineer certain types of citizens and they are used to produce a clean, ordered *folkhemmet*.

And these myriad factors – the difficulty in accessing services; the discouragement from even trying to access services due to the hostility of how they are delivered; the lack of comprehensive and accessible service provision; the experience of discrimination, discipline, conditionality, and social exclusion; the fact that criminalisation, stigma, and discrimination themselves serve to distance people who use drugs from service providers – result in the difficulties for people who use drugs escalating before they seek assistance. Further, people who use drugs may not even seek assistance at all for fear of problematic interactions with service and healthcare providers. Sweden's policies should be seen, as I have stressed, as ones which result, intentionally or not, in harm exacerbation, not harm reduction; the policies make the lives of people who use drugs harder to promote a cessation of drug use.

> 'What we suppose is that the problems are getting deeper for these people before they ask for the help that they need.'
>
> (Interview, RFHL)

The structural violence experienced in Sweden by people who use drugs, fed as it is by discriminatory and generalising preconceptions and assumptions, should be seen in a context of broader social exclusion, oppression, and state-perpetrated violence. I explore these themes in the following chapter.

Notes

1 I should stress that this is not the case only in Sweden: internationally, service and healthcare provision for people who use drugs are often marked by projects of discipline, control, and punishment (INPUD 2015; Keane 2009).

2 Biopower is, 'the more general term for the "power over life" used in [Michel Foucault's (1976)] *The History of Sexuality*' (Dean 1994: 156).

3 One respondent's quotation – quoted in full in the following chapter – is of particular pertinence here, where they noted that people would say '*du är så duktig*' ('you are so good/well behaved') to them in the context of their achievements and/or their cessation of use of drugs.

4 As we may take biopower to be the power over *life*, so we may take geopower to be the power over space, place, and the *earth*. This idea of geopower was – as far as I am aware – conceived and developed by James (Jim) Duncan in a lecture given in the Department of Geography, University of Cambridge, between 2003 and 2006. In subsequent correspondence, he noted that he had (unfortunately) never published the idea.

6 The outcomes of Sweden's war on people who use drugs

This book has focussed on the debates which resulted in Sweden's prohibitionist criminalisation of the use of drugs and the legislation allowing for the compulsory care and treatment of people with drug dependencies. It has explored the legislation's justifying discursive backdrop, and has also focussed on how Swedish discourse and legislation have come to impact service and healthcare provision for people who use drugs, as well as the levels and spaces of drug use in Sweden. I now turn my attention to the outcomes of Sweden's war on people who use drugs, to the real-life outcomes of Sweden's law, policy, and discourse. In this chapter, I examine how the criminalisation of people who use drugs, as well as other laws and policies, and the discourses and understandings that justify them, have impacted the lived experiences and realities of people who use drugs in Sweden.

Topics of stigma and social exclusion will be of specific concentration. These have come to inform the discrimination and violence commonly experienced by people who use drugs. The violence to which people who use drugs are subject is not only structural – notably perpetrated by the institutions discussed in the two preceding chapters – but is also meted out by those charged with protecting Swedish citizens, the Swedish police. The outcomes of Sweden's opposition to various services and healthcare interventions for people who use drugs, particularly harm reduction programmes, will also be discussed in terms of impact upon the health and wellbeing of people who use drugs.

Impacts of the criminalisation of drug use

Stigma

Stigmatisation is a process of social spoiling, where one's identity or social status is tainted or corrupted, as seminally discussed in Goffman's (1968) *Stigma: Notes on the Management of Spoiled Identity*. The social construction and moralisation of people who use drugs internationally – and specifically in Sweden (with these stigmatising constructions being the focus of Chapter 2 of this book) – informs stigma, and requires something by way of (re)introduction since, as is aptly emphasised by Room (2005: 152), '[p]sychoactive substance use occurs in a highly charged field of moral forces'.

Stigmatisation and criminalisation of drug users work together, with the former used to attempt to discourage drug use (Ahern et al. 2007; Room 2005), and the latter justified by the social spoiling accomplished by the former (Ahern et al. 2007), with stigmatisation also – circularly – a consequence of criminalisation. Stigma, in addition to criminalisation, serves to drive people who use drugs underground, acting as a disincentive to seek healthcare and service provision (as we have seen in the previous chapter), and further isolating and alienating people who use drugs from normative society, and reducing opportunities for education, peer-education, organising, empowerment, and outreach and service and healthcare provision, thus exacerbating harm to both people who use drugs and the communities in which they live (Ahern et al. 2007; Degenhardt and Hall 2012; Drucker et al. 1998; Global Commission on Drug Policy 2012). It is no exaggeration to note that stigma kills, since stigma can serve to justify police abuses and general discrimination (Jürgens et al. 2010), as I will discuss in detail towards the end of this chapter, and vulnerability to HIV, hepatitis C, and sexually transmitted/blood-borne infection is accentuated by stigma and discrimination, as well as violence and sexual violence, as is also discussed in this chapter (Logie et al. 2011; WHO 2005b).

Criminalisation is not the only factor driving stigmatisation: what is key is the fact that where an individual uses drugs, they are socially tarnished, irrespective of law (though law certainly does its part to both drive and, circularly, be driven by this tarnishing process). This perspective, that to use 'drugs' is to be, by default, a problematic individual, tells us that those who use drugs are certain 'types' of people (with these pathologising and infantilising stereotypes discussed in Chapter 2), and are not as socially valuable or complete as those who do not use drugs. Ongoing criminalisation, (mis)representation, and conflation of drugs, with little attention to their variable harms or intricacies of consumption, coupled with a medicalisation of addiction as disease (which is discussed again in Chapter 2) (Keane 2002) and 'taken-for-granted connotations of the term "addiction"' (Larkin et al. 2006: 207) – as well as other loaded terminology – feed through into the construction and stigmatisation of people who use drugs themselves, not just of the drugs that they use.

This stigmatisation of people who use drugs is universal but in Sweden is exacerbated by the fact that people who use drugs, who have drugs in their bloodstream, having consumed drugs, are criminal by default in Sweden, where a criminalisation of the very use of drugs has followed from, and in turn fed back into, a characterisation of people who use drugs as untrustworthy, dangerous, and criminal de facto. As discussed in the previous chapter, pathologisation and infantilisation of people who use drugs informs patronising interactions, abuse, exclusion, and punitive disciplining from service providers, and also impacts more general social interactions in civil society.

> 'The criminalisation of the use itself is, I think that's the one that's really causing trouble… if you get caught one, some of these occasions, your life takes another track… it can kind of stigmatise you for life.'
>
> (Interview, RFHL, Drug User)

> 'Because you are stigmatised, once you are, once you have admitted you are a drug user, in any kind of drugs... you are *narkoman* [junkie/drug addict].'
>
> (ibid.)

> 'So many people started [to] say, "oh, you are so good"... and in Sweden, *du är så duktig* [you are so good/well behaved]. In that statement, of course they was trying to say it in a positive way.'
>
> (Interview, Politician – The Left Party; Former Drug User)

People who use drugs in Sweden cannot be honest about their lives and histories, reasonably fearing judgemental response, prejudice, social exclusion, and state-sponsored harassment, arrest, and detention. During the period that I lived and conducted my research in Sweden, the extent to which people who use drugs are problematised in the popular consciousness was clear, recurrent, and commonplace in my general everyday interactions and conversations. With constructions of people who use drugs so endemically negative, and with people who use drugs seen to be unable to exercise agency and self-determination in their decisions due to their pathologisation and infantilisation, those who do not seek assistance with their drug use may even be informed upon by friends, acquaintances, and neighbours, conjuring an image of a repressive nation state that makes use of its citizens in socially engineering a clean, ordered, and disciplined *folkhemmet*.

> 'I have met so many friends during the year[s] who have been in treatment, and tried to create a new life, but they have started to lie, don't tell the new friends about their life.'
>
> (Interview, Politician – The Left Party; Former Drug User)

> 'Because if the neighbours find out that someone [is a drug user], it's very common with anonymous phone calls to the social services.'
>
> (Interview, RFHL, Drug User)

Stigma can be compounded and intersected, with drug-use stigma – what may be termed 'drug-userphobia' – becoming part of a double, triple, or quadruple stigma in the context of (perceived or assumed) sex work, HIV status, and LGBTQ status (Faden et al. 1991; Kayal 1993; UNAIDS 2009). In short, 'overlapping, multilevel forms of stigma and discrimination are representative of an intersectional model of stigma and discrimination' (Logie et al. 2011). And so, with other marginalised communities subject to stigma and discrimination in turn, members of more than one stigmatised communities – sex workers who use drugs, for example – are subject to compound moralisation and stigma internationally, and in Sweden.

> 'Sex work. I think that it's a similar stigma [to drug use], because it's moral, or the source of it often comes from moral opinions... in our society it's, I

think drug users and sex workers are stigmatised partly on that, on the kind of moral judgement.'

(Interview, RFHL, Drug User)

Arrests and fines

Of course, stigma is not the only thing impacting the lived realities of people who use drugs in Sweden: as discussed above it is *criminalisation* that so substantially drives stigma (and stigma in turn that justifies ongoing criminalisation, the two working hand-in-hand to circularly affect the lives of drug users). As discussed in Chapter 1, the Swedish criminalisation of the use of drugs was ostensibly intended (as part of the outspoken and utopian ambition to create a drug-free society) to increase the likelihood of intervention early on during an individual's drug using, in particular designed to prevent young people from continuing with drug use. Indeed, a respondent with the Stockholm Police went so far as to assert that the legislation is not seen to be designed to target and repeatedly harass people who are well-known to the authorities as using drugs, but instead to focus on young people not yet well-known to the authorities:

> 'when they… made this law, the law pointed out that, this is not to be used against old addicts, it's not to be used against people that has been caught several times, this law is to, it's meant to be used against young people… that not has [has not] been detected yet.'
>
> (Interview, Stockholm Police [Narcotics Division Team Leader])

This assertion, however, contrasted starkly with my observation during fieldwork: it is easy for older people who use drugs, including those who are well-known to the authorities and the police, to experience considerable and repeated police intervention, harassment, and violations of bodily integrity by way of urine and blood testing, with resultant accumulations of financial penalties for their drug use (see Van der Giessen and Van Brussel 1996). The above-quoted claim to the contrary was, in fact, described by one key respondent, the Chair and Founder of the Swedish Drug Users Union, as 'bullshit. They (the police) know them by name for God's sake'. A focus on the user means that police can boast a high rate of intervention, using legislation to boost statistics by targeting known people who use drugs in public drug scenes.

> 'In Sweden, the police are using repercussions, I mean, take people into urine tests and etcetera. And they don't do it in Denmark, they don't do it in Norway.'
>
> (Interview, Chair and Founder of *Svenska Brukarföreningen*; Drug User)

> 'The politicians say you have to… take action, and they go to [the] subway, and the *Plattan*, and the police knows a lot of the drug users who is in the area, and then they pick them up, and they take blood samples or urine

samples, and they give them fines, and then you have a record, "We [the police] have done our job". But they are picking [up] people who have had drug problems for ten years… People can have been at the social welfare the same day, and begging for go to treatment… and then you go down and the police pick you up, and take your sample, "Ah, you have used drugs."'

(Interview, Politician – The Left Party; Former Drug User)

'They rather take ten urine samples of drug users and give them finings [fines] for that, than go after one dealer… that's good in the statistics but in the reality they haven't done anything more than ten more drug users got bills to pay that they won't pay, and they got deeper down in misery.'

(Interview, *Svenska Brukarföreningen* Stockholm Coordinator; Former Drug User)

'For their [the police's] statistics, it looks so much better if you have take ten persons that have drugs in the blood, so they harassed us, I think.'

(Interview, Former Sex Worker; Former Drug User)

During fieldwork, I was aware of several occasions when friends, acquaintances, and respondents were subjected to police stops and urine and blood tests as a result of simply 'looking' as if they drug users, thought to be *drogpåverkad* ('under the influence of drugs'), or having *drogögon* ('drug eyes'),[1] with substantial fines resulting from this crime of existing in Sweden as an active drug user. Compulsory testing can be violent and invasive: 'police can go into a bar, merely look one in the eye and arrest him or her, then drag them into police headquarters where blood is extracted from them against their will' (Cohen 2006; also see Hallam 2010):

'the police, they're running around all the restaurants downtown, looking in people's eyes, and they measure the pupils to see, "Oh, you have big pupils, then you must give a urine test, because you could be on cocaine".'

(Interview, Chair and Founder of *Svenska Brukarföreningen*; Drug User)

'Sometimes they just took me because I look, maybe, my eyes looked strange, and they take me to police station just because I have it in my blood, and I get a pay ticket for 2000 crowns, just to have it in the blood.'

(Interview, Former Sex Worker; Former Drug User)

As discussed in Chapter 3, these methods of aesthetic identification of people who use drugs are used to harass and displace people who use drugs from normative public space. Where to 'look' like a drug user or to have 'drug eyes' are arguably spurious, or at least arbitrary and subjectively assessed criteria for identification, they work well in Sweden to justify identification, arrest, violent violation of bodily integrity, and displacement of communities of not only people who use drugs, but also all of those the police use their discretion to so identify. Given the racist moral panics that helped catalyse the introduction of Sweden's contemporary drug legislation, one would be forgiven for wondering what type of person comes to be identified by the Swedish police as 'looking' like they have used drugs – and indeed I discuss this in the *Police* section at the end of this chapter.

Disincentives to seek assistance: losing child custody, compulsory care, criminalisation

People who use drugs who are parents with children in their care in Sweden are, as should now be more than apparent, criminalised and stigmatised as drug users, and can suffer from domestic investigations and intrusions and issues with child custody driven by little more than evidence of drug use (also see *Socialstyrelsen* [National Board of Health and Welfare] 2004). Cases of the authorities intervening in family life, where one or more parent uses drugs, have increased through the mid-late 2000s (EMCDDA 2008). People who use drugs who have children, therefore, have significant disincentive to contact service and healthcare providers and/or the authorities for assistance.

> 'Investigation around your children and your family, that is a big problem, especially for women. Which means women mostly avoid, as long as they possibly can, to get in touch with the authorities telling [them] "I'm a drug addict", because of the children. There is a risk they will take them.'
>
> (Interview, RFHL)

> 'There is a lot of women who have hard drug problems, but who have children… and they know if anyone will know anything, they will lose the children.'
>
> (Interview, Politician – The Left Party; Former Drug User)

Additionally, compulsory care for pregnant women who use drugs was being discussed during the course of fieldwork, 'as a way of protecting the unborn child from injury resulting from the mothers drug use' (EMCDDA 2008: 44). This prioritisation of the welfare of foetuses over that of women has a long history in Sweden and further afield, and although opiate substitution therapy (OST) is recommended by the World Health Organization for women with opiate dependency who are pregnant (WHO/UNODC/UNAIDS 2004), criminalising and stigmatising pregnant people who use drugs (compounded by the fear of state interventions and the possible loss of the custody of the child when it is born) serves to act as a disincentivising barrier for pregnant women to seek assistance, distancing individuals who are in great need of medical assistance (or OST, for example) from the authorities and healthcare providers:

> 'they don't realise that women with drug problems, who get pregnant, will never go to the healthcare, and use all that kind of help, that other women get.'
>
> (Interview, Politician – The Left Party; Former Drug User)

Further acting as hindrance and barrier to support and service and healthcare provision, seeking assistance for drug-related issues involves 'coming out' (and being registered) as a drug user, which may present difficulties in terms of housing and employment. It is clear the extent to which stigma and criminalisation drive social exclusion of people who use drugs in Sweden, thus in turn distancing them from the services they require.

> 'Less people are getting the help they need in time. Because they not, they don't feel trust for the system enough to go there and ask for that help... people who get involved with the police for being drug addicts, they don't get jobs.'
>
> (Interview, RFHL)

> 'I want to educate to be a nurse or something like that, and maybe in the hospitals they don't want to have drug users... it's a bit hard to get back if you want to change your life and have a real job and live a legal life.'
>
> (Interview, Former Sex Worker; Former Drug User)

Stigma, fines, domestic intrusions, and prison, all act as substantial disincentives for people who use drugs to seek assistance, tallying with Darke and Hall's (2003: 193) observation that 'the most common reason given for delaying seeking help is fear of police involvement'. Calling an ambulance for a drug-related emergency such as overdose can result in attendance of police and ensuing blood and/or urine tests and prosecutions. People may also be unwilling to come to the assistance of individuals in medical difficulty due to drug consumption, again for fear of facing legal ramification by association. In Sweden, it seems, it is not only drug use that drives social exclusion, but also associations with those who may have used drugs; stigma is 'sticky'.

> 'If I overdose, and my friends call 911 for help... the ambulance came, but also the police, because it is a crime to take drugs... they also check up all of the other people present. And that's a reason for a drug user to not phone 911. And because of that people die.'
>
> (Interview, *Svenska Brukarföreningen* Stockholm Coordinator; Former Drug User)

> 'So many people will avoid to get help or to seek the healthcare because they are afraid that they will be, that the healthcare will tell the police and everything, so they keep away.'
>
> (Interview, Politician – The Left Party; Former Drug User)

> 'There was one person who lay down in *tunelbanan* [the subway] where you wait for a *tunelbana* [subway train]... [on the] platform, he lay down... The person... you know, step over him... Because they think, okay, oh maybe he had drugs on [him], in the pockets.'
>
> (Interview, Former Drug User)

Results of 'harm exacerbation' policies

Increased difficulties for people who use drugs result from criminalising legislation, and stigma, which serve to deter people who use drugs from seeking assistance and healthcare and service provision. This is compounded by Sweden's stance on service provision and harm reduction services, particularly policies of service providers allowing harm to escalate through an active withholding of services – what I have termed 'harm exacerbation' (see Chapters 4 and 5).

High threshold methadone

As discussed in the previous chapter, people who use drugs frequently experience difficulties gaining access, and retaining access, to opiate substitution therapy programmes in Sweden, with people kicked off opiate substitution for using (any) other drugs, for problematised behaviour, and a plethora of other reasons. This is concerning, as disqualification from such programmes frequently results in people recommencing use of black-market opiates (also see Drucker et al. 1998), with higher likelihood of overdose and death due to reductions in opiate tolerance that occur during substitution therapy (Davoli et al. 2007; Strang et al. 2003), and additionally due to the fact that it is often impossible to ascertain the purity of drugs bought on a black market. Indeed, Sweden's strikingly high overdose mortality rate, discussed in Chapter 3, exists in this context of high threshold substitution programmes, disqualification from programmes, and general opposition to harm reduction (discussed in Chapters 4 and 5).

> '[They are ejected from opiate substitution therapy] because they used other substances. And then they solve it to [by] take[ing] the methadone away… they relapse on heroin of course. And a lot of them overdose and die and the clinics know all this… You are like blocked for six months… Because take the methadone away from a *heroinist* [heroin user], my guess is that 100 percent relapse on heroin.'
>
> (Interview, *Svenska Brukarföreningen* Stockholm Coordinator; Former Drug User)

Some of those who have lost, or have been unable to gain, access to substitution therapy are forced to obtain methadone or buprenorphine illegally on the black market from drug dealers, or from acquaintances who now require a lower dose than prescribed. People who use drugs in Sweden are thus again forced to fill the gaps themselves in service and healthcare provision.

> 'She like gets methadone from friends, [she] is trying to cut off the heroin use, and I think she is successful… for her it's another universe, her life is possible because of this illegal methadone.'
>
> (Interview, *Svenska Brukarföreningen* Stockholm Coordinator; Former Drug User)

> 'That *indicates methadone bottle* will cost me, in the streets, this bottle can be like 500 crowns [approx. £50GBP], so that should be, yeah, then I have to start at prostitution again, just to have methadone. So that's, yeah, that's totally insane.'
>
> (Interview, Former Sex Worker; Former Drug User)

When the last respondent quoted here gained access to black market methadone, it allowed her to cease selling sex to acquire heroin (also see Drucker et al. 1998; Gibson et al. 1999). Having high thresholds for participation on opiate substitution programmes can therefore prolong sex work undertaken to fund black market opiate use and acquisition, quite at odds with Swedish outspoken aspirations to eliminate sex work (which I discuss elsewhere [Levy 2015]). As these respondents noted:

> 'if you are paying for your drugs by being in prostitution, then you can't stop being a prostitute'.
>
> (Interview, Inger Segelström, Politician – Social Democrats)

> 'My friend on the street, she didn't want to work with this [sex work], she hated it, but she was using heroin, and she was waiting to get in the programme for Subutex. And after she was having Subutex, she left the business, starting to work with her ordinary work, and some people don't want to give people Subutex, but now she have a life, and before she was very sad.'
>
> (Interview, Sex Worker)

Illegal needles, needle sharing, and needle reusing

Due to the policy environment in which they use drugs, people who inject drugs in Sweden can experience significant difficulties when it comes to safely injecting. Although the UNODC (2006: 16) states that 'harm reduction measures were implemented in areas where they were needed' in Sweden, this is *entirely* inconsistent with the experiences of people who inject drugs in Sweden. It is not overstatement to emphasise that this assertion of the UNODC is entirely misleading. As noted, only two official needle and syringe programmes existed nationally at the time of fieldwork, and it is illegal for people who use drugs to buy needles and injecting paraphernalia from shops and pharmacies.

Due to these substantive barriers in accessing the services with which to reduce drug-related harms, people who use drugs in Sweden report having to buy needles at extortionate rates from drug dealers, from friends, and from pharmacies in Denmark (also see Ljungberg et al. 1991). Needles are also imported and/or stolen, highlighting the lengths to which people who use drugs have to go as a result of the state's failure to provide harm reduction services, starkly contrary to the UNODC's above assertion. Respondents also noted sharing needles and a black market for buying *used* needles, with the use of such needles and injecting paraphernalia increasing the risk of the transmission of blood-borne infections, other infections, cosmetic and vascular damage, and again unambiguously highlighting the enormous difficulties faced in obtaining injection kit and Sweden's failure to provide adequate harm reduction. Unable to acquire new, sterile needles, people who use drugs in Sweden are forced to use and reuse their needles for long periods, causing significant vascular and cosmetic damage, and infections.

> 'I saved my own [needles]. Months and months and months, I think for years sometimes... And you share with friends. There is a black market for used needles in Sweden. One of our members came here and he told us that the same morning... with a guy he don't know – he just met him – and they put their money together and buy heroin. And then he found out that "Oh, I have no needles", and he asked that unknown guy if he could buy his. He like take [took] it out of his system and just "Here, please. Five euro"... [Needles are obtained via] burglary from veterinarian and local doctors. They, like, buy it from other countries.'
>
> (Interview, *Svenska Brukarföreningen* Stockholm Coordinator; Former Drug User)

> 'You can pay up to 100 crowns for a syringe, and a needle, and yeah, like people use it for weeks and change to [exchange with] other people, and it spreads diseases and it's so bad... I have done it many times, I took someone else's needle... three weeks ago I made [took] this blood test for HIV and *hepatit* [hepatitis], so I just hope it's negative.'
>
> (Interview, Former Sex Worker; Former Drug User)

> 'Sometimes, I had the same needle for three weeks, but that was when my veins was better... one time, I sit in [for] three hours just to sit and try everywhere, and all the arms are just bleeding.'
>
> (ibid.)

Needle sharing was even *advocated* by a representative of prohibitionist organisation RNS – the organisation responsible for heavily influencing the shape of Sweden's drug legislation, policy, and discourse (see Chapter 1), and who staunchly oppose needle and syringe programmes (see Chapter 4) – as well as other Swedish stakeholders (see Amundsen et al. 2003), who suggested that people living with HIV should share a needle after those who are HIV negative. Aside from their brazen dismissal of well-proven blood-borne infection prevention interventions and opposition to the provision of means with which to improve the health and welfare of people who use drugs, such suggestions also fail to engage with the time taken to seroconvert (i.e. develop detectible HIV antibodies in the bloodstream, with some HIV tests testing only for HIV antibodies), whilst assuming *all* people who inject drugs are aware of their serostatus. Moreover, such suggestions entirely fail to engage with hepatitis C – the most important blood-borne infection impacting people who inject drugs – and other health and wellbeing implications of sharing injecting paraphernalia.

> 'You can even share needles with HIV positive people. That's possible to do. If you and I would have one needle, and you're positive and I'm not, you take last. It's as simple as that.'
>
> (Interview, RNS)

As discussed in this book's Introduction, when infected with a communicable disease, the Swedish Communicable Disease Act requires an individual to behave in such a way as to conform to behaviours ostensibly designed to protect the Swedish community at large, which would include avoiding needle sharing if one knows that one is living with HIV, for example (Baldwin 2005). A lack of, and opposition to, needle and syringe provision, which results in people who use drugs being forced to share injecting paraphernalia, can therefore be seen to be at odds with Sweden's 'contain and control' HIV policy, preventing those who inject from abiding by the Communicable Disease Act, and thus putting themselves and others at risk of blood-borne infections, and therefore running the risk of medical isolation under the Act.

> 'According to the law for those who are infected with HIV, they have to behave safe. They haven't got a choice, but they are not given the possibility to live safe, as they don't have the possibility to get the needles.'
>
> (Interview, Chair of RFHL)

Blood-borne infections

HIV incidence and prevalence in Sweden, and amongst people who inject drugs in Sweden, are lower than in Europe overall (UNODC 2006: 50), and this has always been the case: a brief increase in HIV infections amongst people who inject drugs in 2007 – suggesting 'the continued potential for HIV outbreaks among injecting drug users' (EMCDDA 2009: 80) – appeared to stabilise at previous levels of around 21 annual cases (EMCDDA 2008).

However, a focus on HIV/AIDS has served to peripheralise a focus on hepatitis C (see Rhodes 2004),[2] a very readily transmitted blood-borne infection, and the most important infection affecting people who inject drugs (Health Protection Agency et al. 2008; UNODC 2011), since the sharing of needles *and* the sharing of other injection paraphernalia facilitates its spread. A lack of education about how to inject safely, about the nature of hepatitis C, compounded by a lack of provision of sterile injecting and drug using paraphernalia and needles and syringes, have all contributed to a strikingly high hepatitis C prevalence amongst Sweden's communities of people who inject drugs.

> 'Everyone is talking about HIV, and for us, the drug users, hepatitis C is a much bigger problem… during the last three years, seven of my friends have passed away from hepatitis C.'
>
> (Interview, Chair and Founder of *Svenska Brukarföreningen*; Drug User)

In the past, people who inject drugs have made up around two thirds of people living with hepatitis C in Sweden (Van der Giessen and Van Brussel 1996). In 2008, 1,071 of 2,520 (over 42%) of new hepatitis C cases with known transmission were amongst people who inject drugs (EMCDDA 2010). Limited testing in 1994 estimated 91% of people in Sweden who inject drugs were infected with hepatitis C (WHO 2004), with other figures suggesting 90% (Home Affairs Minutes of Evidence 2002) and more recent testing of 310 people who inject drugs in Stockholm noting 86.5% prevalence (Lidman et al. 2009). Recently, incidence of hepatitis C among people in Sweden who inject drugs was estimated by the Swedish Institute for Infectious Disease Control at 95% within two years of injecting (Hallam 2010), with other estimates at around 25% after one year, and 50% after two years, highlighting the necessity for 'early intervention efforts' (Lidman et al. 2009: 679). These prevalence and incidence estimates are strikingly higher than the global mean average of 45.2–55.3% amongst people who inject drugs (UNODC 2011), and higher than, for example, the UK prevalence of around 50% (Advisory Council on the Misuse of Drugs 2009; Health Protection Agency et al. 2008). Highlighting the impact of the (lack of) availability of sterile needles and syringes and harm reduction interventions, Norden et al. (2013: 3–4) emphasise that hepatitis C prevalence in Stockholm (prior to the very recent introduction of the Stockholm needle and syringe programme) was almost double that in Rotterdam, Netherlands, and further that the

> 'main difference between the two cities was that the participants from Stockholm significantly more often shared needles and syringes. They also shared other paraphernalia significantly more often… The IDUs [injecting drug users] in Rotterdam have had full access to NSPs [needle and syringe programmes] and well-developed OST [opiate substitution therapy] since about 2 decades, whereas in Stockholm, IDUs have no access to NSPs.'
>
> (ibid.)

Respondents from RFHL and *Svenska Brukarföreningen* discussed a remarkable prevalence of hepatitis C in Sweden, quoting statistics ranging from 80% to 98% prevalence.

> 'I got hepatitis C, like more than 90% of the Swedish people who inject drugs… they told me that I am starting to get a [liver] cirrhosis… I have like the worst type [of hepatitis C] of course, that less than 50% get well after one year with interferon… Because I shared needles, and there is no prevention [for hepatitis C].'
>
> (Interview, *Svenska Brukarföreningen* Stockholm Coordinator; Former Drug User)

> 'For a short time, you can provide it [clean needles] for yourself if you are lucky… but if you use drugs for like 10, 20, 30 years, there will be situations when you don't have your own clean needles.'
>
> (ibid.)

Hepatitis C infection seems inevitable when injecting in a state where sterile needles and injecting paraphernalia are so difficult to acquire. The only way for people who inject drugs to avoid blood-borne infections in Sweden appears to be a cessation of injecting drug use: those who continue are expected to 'take the consequences' of their drug use and of Sweden's harm exacerbation policies.

> 'it's a moral issue, it's a bad behaviour. People should not use drugs. People should quit. Why should society provide that [needles]? You have the problem. You have the behaviour. You take the consequences of the behaviour.'
>
> (Interview, RNS)

> '[there is an idea that] "we can't say yes to needle exchange programmes, because it's not legal to use drugs in Sweden". So then you lose your humanity, you don't give a damn about what the research is telling you, you don't give a damn that we have people dying because they should stop [not] use the drug.'
>
> (Interview, Chair of RFHL)

> JAY: 'If someone is an injecting drug user… how would they not get hepatitis?'
>
> RESPONDENT: 'By not, just not using'.
>
> (Interview, IOGT-NTO; Previously RNS)

These strikingly high figures of incidence and prevalence of hepatitis C amongst people who inject drugs do not appear to concern Swedish authorities who, as discussed, remain staunchly in support of Swedish prohibition and thus of policies which drive the spread of blood-borne infections. With hepatitis C so predominantly affecting a group who are both demonised and criminalised, it may well be that, as with HIV/AIDS in the 1980s and early 1990s, 'only when the "general public" is threatened can whatever the opposite of a general public is hope to get adequate attention and treatment' (Bersani 1988: 203).

> 'Because there are mostly drug users who have it [hepatitis C], it's not a priority. It has no priority.'
>
> (Interview, RFHL)

> 'Because it's mostly drug users that get it. And you know that drug use is illegal. And so you have yourself to blame.'
>
> (Interview, RFHL, Drug User)

Ineligibility for hepatitis C treatment

Consistent with other exclusions, in spite of such high prevalence amongst people who inject drugs, respondents noted that people who use drugs have been turned away from potentially life-saving interferon treatment for hepatitis C.[3] Although opiate use and opiate substitution therapy do not affect the success of interferon treatment (Bruggmann et al. 2007), people who use drugs are discriminatorily and assumptively generalised as being too unreliable to attend appointments with the punctuality necessary for successful treatment (see quotations below).

> 'If you have an appointment, they usually don't come when they have an appointment, they come at the wrong hours.'
>
> (Interview, Psychiatrist working with drug addiction; Previously with RNS)

> 'If you are an active drug user, you don't get interferon... they say that you wouldn't come to the doctors' appointment, you will miss your times... But if they really want to help us, then of course they shouldn't deny us treatment for hepatitis C on that basis... they really block you out from life-saving treatments.'
>
> (Interview, *Svenska Brukarföreningen* Stockholm Coordinator; Former Drug User)

> 'They who has the most difficult life, with the biggest unfulfilled needs. They who are without homes, they who don't get paid by social security, they with the biggest problems, they add to that, that they don't get healthcare as well... It fits, if you can see how they treat these people in other contexts, it fits the picture that they don't get healthcare either.'
>
> (ibid.)

Such understandings seem driven by those crude conflations and generalisations that mark the pathologising and infantilising social constructions of people who use drugs as unreliable and disordered. Given that people who use drugs are so heavily demonised, stigmatised, and criminalised in Sweden, it seems something of a self-serving and self-fulfilling prophecy to create an infrastructure that socially excludes and disrupts the lives of these marginalised communities, and then associates the outcomes of those very same exclusions and disruptions reductively only with their drug use.

Such healthcare provision for treating hepatitis C is furthermore seen as something of a lost cause in Sweden: as the means (sterile needles, syringes, and injecting paraphernalia) with which to avoid hepatitis C are, by and large, unavailable, it is simply assumed that people who inject drugs will inevitably be re-infected through their continuing drug use in an infrastructure that does little to reduce the risks associated with said drug use, thus negating any long term success of treatment. In short (and circularly), Swedish drug policies have made hepatitis C infection almost inevitable for people who inject drugs, and then this inevitability is used to explain the contrived futility of treating those who are infected.

> 'You will not get interferon treatment, you know, they won't take it away [the hepatitis] unless you've been free of drugs for two years... they say "I mean,

that won't do any good, because if you still out there taking drugs, you will get it [hepatitis] again. So it's a waste money, time".'

(Interview, RFHL, Drug User)

The refusal to treat people who use drugs for hepatitis C is striking, given that an estimated 75–85% of those infected may develop chronic infection, potentially leading to liver cirrhosis, liver cancer, and liver failure (Degenhardt and Hall 2012; Health Protection Agency et al. 2008), with infection representing 'a major cause of morbidity' (Patrick et al. 2001) and, indeed, mortality: after 20 years of infection, 7% may develop cirrhosis, 20% after 40 years (Degenhardt and Hall 2012). People who inject drugs who are unwilling or unable to change their behaviour are, nonetheless, not entitled to this treatment.

People who use drugs and the Swedish police and security forces

> [A]n approach to drug use that is primarily the responsibility of law enforcement officials rather than health care personnel results in corruption, abuses, and reluctance on the part of drug users to access even the most basic disease prevention services.
>
> (Open Society Institute 2009: 7)

> 'Violations committed in the name of drug control… reported from all regions worldwide, are abhorrent and must be combated.'
>
> (Jürgens et al. 2010: 482)

Globally, the so-called 'war on drugs' has resulted in a state-sponsored and police-driven war on people who use drugs (Buchanan and Young 2000; Open Society Institute 2009), in turn fuelling drug production- and trafficking-related violence (Global Commission on Drug Policy 2012; Reuter and Trautmann 2007). Criminalisation, stigmatisation, and discrimination against people who use drugs (and the drugs they use), all of which form the foundation upon which prohibition rests by attempting to control and supress drug use, have been of substantial detriment to the welfare and health of people who use drugs, as well as the communities in which they live (Degenhardt and Hall 2012; Des Jarlais 1995; Global Commission on Drug Policy 2012; INPUD 2015): people who use drugs face violence, executions, extrajudicial killings, incarcerations, abuse, and discrimination from the police and state, and in civil society (Jürgens et al. 2010; Open Society Institute 2009). And so in Sweden, it is perhaps unsurprising that people who use drugs, people who are heavily criminalised, stigmatised, and socially excluded, experience difficulties with the police, all the more unsurprising in a context of their experiencing difficulties with service and healthcare providers, institutional and physical violence, and stigma as a result of prohibitionist laws and discourses.

Interactions between the Swedish police and security forces and civilians are by no means uniform or consistent when it comes to marginalised groups in Sweden. The Swedish police have, in recent years, come under fire for misconduct and abuse, and the racism which is apparently endemic in some forces (notably the Rosengård area of Malmö, where racial tension and civil unrest have been recurrent problems) has been cause for considerable concern (*The Local* 2009; also see below respondent quotations). All the more concerning in the context of the topics explored in this book is that Swedish understandings and social constructions of drug use and people who use drugs has, during the course of the drug debate in Sweden, intersected with racist and xenophobic generalisations and moral panics of threats of 'foreign' drugs, 'foreign' drug using practices and patterns, and 'foreign' communities. All of this has informed and racialised Swedish drugs discourse. I have, indeed, elsewhere discussed police abuse, unprofessionalism, and allegations of violence in police interactions with other marginalised communities in Sweden (Levy 2015).

> 'There are bad cops, I mean, everywhere, and that that happens also with drug users and immigrants; we just had, you probably heard, the situation in Malmö, Rosengård. There has been some violence in one of the suburbs of Malmö, and policeman sitting in the car screaming, saying really, really bad stuff, like, racist stuff, that they [the immigrants] are monkeys.'
>
> (Interview, IOGT-NTO; Previously RNS)

> 'I think the police has, they look down on the prostitute… It's the same, that the Swedish police look down at the drug users, and every person who's not normal, the police look down on.'
>
> (Interview, Politician – Social Democrats)

It seems that groups which have been constructed as deviant and socially disruptive are simply not regarded by the police and state as being entitled to the same state-sponsored police protections as afforded to other citizens in Sweden's *folkhemmet*.

Good intentions?

Swedish drug policy focusses on people who use drugs themselves, through criminalising drug *use* in itself. This high degree of focus on people who use drugs was criticised by a respondent from the Stockholm Police Narcotics Division, though he emphasised that police officers working with people who use drugs were motivated compassionately, not punitively (despite legislation's ample room for punitive application). Indeed, it is officially argued in Sweden that emphasis on people who use drugs 'is not viewed in punitive terms by its advocates, but rather as providing protection, assistance and support' (Hallam 2010: 2).

> 'Swedish police has rightfully, I think, been criticised in recent years, for focussing too much on the user level, and not so much at the supply level.'
>
> (Interview, Stockholm Police [Narcotics Division Team Leader])

> 'The most police officers [who I know] that work against drugs, we are very human-loving people. We, our motivation is that the tragedy, the human tragedy with using drugs, and most police officers that I know, it's not in our interest to punish people'.
>
> (ibid.)

Yet in spite of being motivated by the 'human tragedy' of drug use, state responses are not – as I hope to have made very clear – sympathetic or empowering: responses take, instead, the form of severe penalties, involving, as has been discussed, fines, incarceration, domestic intrusions, abuses, as well as the possibility of compulsory treatment.

Difficulties in reporting crime

As explored in this chapter, people who use drugs are disinclined to contact healthcare providers and emergency services for fear of police involvement and resultant drug testing, detention and/or incarceration, and/or fining. This reluctance is compounded by widespread disrepute of the police amongst communities of people who use drugs and drug user rights organisations. As with other marginalised communities in Sweden (Levy 2015), drug user respondents reported difficulties in leaving statements with the police once their drug user status became apparent, an institutionalised prejudice against individuals who are, by definition, criminalised.

> 'Talked with a girl today, a user herself who's been hit by a guy, you know. Face bleeding… And the police came… they realised that she was an addict, because she's very good looking and so on it's not that obvious you know, they just said "Oh, you're an addict. We just hate addicts, I can't stand addicts. So splash off the blood from your face and get the hell out."'
>
> (Interview, RFHL, Drug User)

With drug use criminalised, people who use drugs are vulnerable to police abuses and violence – which were recurrent themes during my interviews and fieldwork – with a representative of drug user rights organisation, RFHL, noting such abuses to be commonplace. Security guards, some of whom are entitled to carry nightsticks and handcuffs, work with relative impunity from police intervention, and I have been informed of several occasions, observing one myself, of these guards assaulting individuals with police complicity and witness.

> 'With the Securitas [guards], yeah of course they harass, they really harass drug users. Of course they do… the Securitas people also file complaints against you often, and they, the Securitas [are] two persons, and the drug user is alone, and it comes to a matter of proof.'
>
> (Interview, Chair and Founder of *Svenska Brukarföreningen*; Drug User)

A police refusal to take statements concerning authorities' abuses was exemplified during an instance of assault that I witnessed in 2010, where a security guard crushed an individual's face into the pavement while he remained restrained by another guard. There were between five and ten police in the vicinity, several of whom witnessed the incident, none of whom intervened. I spoke to five officers before I found one who did not refuse to take my statement.

Violence

People who use drugs in Sweden are not only criminalised, but are socially constructed as deviant, dangerous, disruptive, unreliable, violent, and threatening to the normative social order of the Swedish *folkhemmet* nation state. Such stigmatising understandings of this marginalised community feed through into their experiencing considerable violence from the Swedish authorities.

With no drug consumption rooms in Sweden, people who inject drugs can be forced to inject in public or semi-public spaces, but do so at great risk to their health – with such drug use often being marked by a need to rush injection, the increased risk of needle and paraphernalia sharing and blood-borne infection, difficulties in maintaining hygiene, and by the risk of violence perpetrated by the community or the police and security forces. An example was given of an individual who was attacked by security staff after overdosing in a public toilet in Stockholm's Central Station:

> 'he was at the toilet at Central Station, and took heroin in an injection, and took an overdose, and fell to the floor. And he woke up by one of the security guards sitting on him, and smashing, like this, in the face... He managed to hit the security guard, you know. Not hard... And they all four started to kick him. Kicked out all his teeth in his upper jaw.'
>
> (Interview, RFHL, Drug User)

With drug use criminalised, simply the act of 'walking around looking like a drug addict' (see below quotation) can be reason for intervention and violence. The above-quoted respondent also referred to a couple, known to be people who use drugs, who were assaulted by security guards in the *Gallerian* mall, next to *Plattan*. Similarly to the above instances, they were not permitted to press charges, and were accused of 'starting a fire and smashing a window' when they attempted to report the assault, the police seemingly granting the security guards immunity from prosecution.

> 'The security guards or whatever they're called, took her and her boyfriend downstairs and said that they had been smoking there... they started to abuse her, not him, at the end four of these guys were standing and kicking at her when she was laying at the floor... they were... standing and kicking her, when the police came to the scene... the fourth one just kept on... screaming "You fucking *pundar hora* [junkie whore]"... they [the police] didn't charge any of these guys.'
>
> (Interview, RFHL, Drug User)

> 'And they hadn't been doing anything wrong, you know. Just going and walking around looking like a drug addict.'
>
> (ibid.)

These reports of violence bear similarity to the well-known violent arrest and death of Osmo Vallo in Sweden in 1995. Vallo had been reported to the police for supposedly being under the influence of drugs and/or alcohol and he died after having been restrained by police, who – during the process of restraining him – stamped on his back and kicked him repeatedly (Amnesty International 1997). With Vallo's death in police custody being more than two decades ago, it seems that Swedish police and security forces continue to perpetrate acts of violence on people who use drugs, and continue to do so with apparent impunity.

Summary: exacerbated harm, danger, and violence for people who use drugs

Political debates prior to the introduction of laws criminalising the use of drugs and allowing for the compulsory treatment of people with drug dependency emphasised that the laws should not be used punitively against people who use drugs. Rather, it was argued that the enforcement of Sweden's prohibitionist legislation would serve as means for intervention and assistance for people who use drugs, and that the legislation would not be used in a wanton or repressive fashion.

However, the enforcement of these laws on the ground certainly cannot be said to have assisted the people who use drugs in Sweden. Far from it: as a result of Sweden's pursuit of punitive prohibition, people who use drugs have actually experienced exacerbated stigma, discrimination, social exclusion, threats to health and wellbeing, and violence and abuse. Moreover, Sweden's prohibitionist discourse has served to inform opposition to healthcare and service provision that would suitably and comprehensively meet the needs of people who use drugs (particularly harm reduction services) and has resulted in causing substantial harm to those people. Notably, this includes very high hepatitis C prevalence, a lack of access to hepatitis C treatment for people who continue using drugs, and difficulties in acquiring and maintaining access to opiate substitution therapy. Furthermore, stigma and criminalisation have worked hand-in-hand in legitimising and driving difficulties, violence, and abuse at the hands of the Swedish police

And state-sponsored violence, criminalisation, and threats of arrest and incarceration all serve as barriers in Sweden to people who use drugs seeking assistance from the authorities and from service and healthcare providers. Swedish drugs law, policy, and discourse have had catastrophic outcomes for the lives and lived experiences of people who use drugs in Sweden.

Notes

1 *Drogögon* is a phrase popularised by the Swedish Prime Minister 2006–2014, Fredrik Reinfeldt.

2 A UNODC (2006) report discusses low Swedish drug user HIV prevalence; however, it omits any involved discussion of hepatitis C (also see Amundsen 2003), HIV seemingly coming to eclipse a focus on more pressing and pertinent health concerns for many people who use drugs.

3 DAA, Direct Acting Antiviral medication (such as Sofosbuvir), is used to treat hepatitis C more effectively than, and without the same side-effects as, interferon. It had, however, not yet been rolled out for treatment of hepatitis C at the time of my fieldwork and research, with approval only coming at the end of 2013, and the drug being launched in 2014.

Conclusions

Harm exacerbation, social exclusion, and violence

Sweden has adopted staunchly repressive drug legislation, criminalising the use of drugs and allowing for compulsory treatment for those with drug and alcohol dependency. The focus of this book has been on the drug laws of Sweden, on establishing the results of these laws, these laws' realisation as policy on the ground, and on the discursive backdrop of Sweden's prohibitionist legislation.

And so, what have been the outcomes of Sweden's quest for a 'drug-free society'? What has been the outcome of Sweden's criminalisation of the use of drugs and compulsory treatment for drug users? This concluding chapter summarises the findings of my research and fieldwork, and emphasises that Sweden's prohibitionist drugs legislation has had substantial and substantively negative impacts on the lives and lived realities of people who use drugs in Sweden. It emphasises that though Sweden is oft perceived as a bastion of liberal, inclusive, and progressive democracy, as the ultimate welfare state, this reputation is misleading, both in terms of Sweden's history, and in terms of how Sweden continues to police, contain, and control marginalised and demonised communities who are seen to pose a threat to the fabric of the Swedish nation state.

Summary of research: the Swedish model of drug prohibition

Silencing; pathologisation; displacement

I have stressed and restressed that Sweden's drug legislation must be seen in the context of Sweden's historical and ongoing projects of containment and control of communities seen to threaten the Swedish *folkhemmet* or 'People's Home'. Sweden's legislation criminalising the use of drugs and allowing for the compulsory treatment and medicalised detention of those with drug and alcohol dependencies were not introduced in a vacuum, and are not in stark contrast to an otherwise 'liberal' state. Far from it. Sweden has a long history of social control, exclusion, and projects of containing and controlling populations constructed as deviant and dangerous, seen to be a threat to normative social order. Sweden's aspirations to create a clean and orderly *folkhemmet* have, in fact, resulted in sex workers, women, people who use drugs and alcohol, those with disabilities, foreign nationals, people of colour, and/or those seen to be eugenically deficient all being subject to violent and repressive legislative and policy interventions, including sterilisations, compulsory medical inspections, and medicalised incarcerations and detentions without trial at times during the 19th and 20th centuries.

Sweden's social engineering projects were notably extensive, coercive, and violent through the 19th and 20th centuries; where these were justified by playing upon concerns surrounding groups that ostensibly threatened to destabilise the Swedish nation state, so too was Sweden's criminalisation of the use of drugs justified in the late 1980s. These concerns included moral panics surrounding the spread of HIV/AIDS from marginal (and marginalised) populations constructed as deviant and dangerous – notably, people who use drugs and sex workers – to the normative populace, coupled with racialised and xenophobic panics pertaining to the perceived threat of the spread of HIV from migrant (read: non-white) populations to the (hetero)normative Swedish (read: white) population, and were associated also with fears of the rise and influx of 'foreign' and 'un-Swedish' drugs and patterns and cultures of drug use. These racist and drug-userphobic concerns were ever present in popular and media discourse, and informed the legal debates which preceded the 1988 criminalising legislation in Sweden through the 1970s and 1980s. The debates were therefore marked by a focus on ***demand***, a focus on people who use drugs themselves as being the fundamental element of a pyramid of drug use: eliminate demand through criminalising drug users and their very *use* of drugs, and supply and drug trafficking would become irrelevant. Since, however, Sweden's moral panic has been precipitated by fears of the foreign and foreign drugs, various substances viewed as traditionally Swedish have remained for the most part exempt from concern and from criminalisation: snus oral tobaccos, a quintessentially Swedish psychoactive drug, remains legal despite commercial banning in the EU, and alcohol consumption is also normalised in Sweden (despite its extremely popular prevalence), all whilst Sweden continues its (selective and arguably xenophobically motivated) crusade against un-Swedish psychoactive drugs and un-Swedish patterns of drug use in attempts to create a (very selectively defined) 'drug-free society'.

Though Swedish political debates allow for numerous interested parties to contribute, the meaningful participation of people who use drugs in the legal debate has been sidelined, silenced, and invisiblised. This has been achieved through an undermining of the testimony of people who use drugs, particularly those with drug dependencies, who are generalised as having a disease of 'addiction', with this disease claimed as undermining their agency and self-determination, and being marked by 'symptoms' that include a combination of pathology and passivity, and deceptive and dangerous criminality. In short, such understandings have rendered the input and contribution of people who use drugs as moot and dismissible. Not only are people who use drugs seen to be pathological and infantile, rendered as incapable through their drug use and their addictions, but their very *use* of drugs is also seen in Sweden to be a type of infectious disease, with the use of drugs passed from one drug user on to the uninitiated. This idea of drug use itself as a type of social and transmissible sickness is peculiar to Sweden, and has been promoted by those very stakeholders who have so conspicuously and influentially informed the

Swedish drugs debates. These constructions of drug users as diseased and their drug use itself as another disease have been used not only to justify the exclusion and silencing of communities and organisations of people who use drugs, but also to justify Sweden's drug legislation: with people who use drugs undermined as unreliable, sick, deviant, and dangerous, and their drug use constructed as a transmissible infection, people who use drugs have come to be the absolute focus of Sweden's drug law and policy. With agency and self-determination undermined, the compulsory treatment and medicalised detention of people who use drugs follows, as does the criminalisation of their drug use. Both of these laws must be seen to have been enacted paternalistically, the Swedish state caring for its recalcitrant children who do not know how to care for themselves. Elsewhere in the EU and Western Europe, such a staunchly punitive and criminalising focus would be contentious, but by the exclusion of various parties in the drug debate, Sweden has been successful in establishing both a consensus on drug policy, and a dominant discourse that justifies such interventions.

Swedish drug legislation is designed to create a drug-free society, and though some stakeholders boast that Sweden has low levels of drug use, it seems that Sweden's laws have had little demonstrable impact on *levels* of drug use, which have always been relatively low, and have not diminished in any considerable way following the introduction of the legislation. Instead, Swedish drug law and policy have had considerable impacts on the *spaces and spatial dynamics* of drug use. Sweden's criminalisation of the use of drugs has been favoured by police and policy makers as a means with which to displace drug users from public space and civil society, to sanitise urban areas and to move drug users and drug use into clandestine space. People who use drugs have not only been displaced, therefore, from contribution to drugs debate: they have actually been physically displaced as well. Swedish policies have historically been marked by their spatial focus, and the same is the case with contemporary drug policy.

Such displacement strategies often serve to exacerbate difficulties and dangers for marginalised communities since they increase the distances between those communities and service and healthcare providers, but they have been favoured here – much as Sweden has historically favoured displacement and spatial and social cleansing. As with Sweden's history of violent social engineering and control of marginalised communities, Sweden's drug legislation must be seen in the context of Sweden's history of using legislation – notable examples being Sweden's HIV/AIDS and communicable disease legislation, and Sweden's vagrancy legislation – as a mechanism with which to contain, control, and curtail the movements of said communities whilst protecting the normative population from the aesthetical and moral dangers they are felt to pose.

The outcomes of law and policy: service provision, harm exacerbation, and violence

With Sweden displacing and invisiblising drugs and the people who use them – both in political discourse and debate, and in literal, spatial terms – the ideas that frame and justify Sweden's drug legislation have had considerable and negative effects upon the ideas of service and healthcare providers. Sweden's outspoken desire to create a drug-free society has resulted in opposition to harm reduction interventions, with services designed to reduce the harms that can be associated with drug use dismissed by many key stakeholders and service and healthcare providers as promoting, endorsing, and facilitating drug use. Needle and syringe programmes are few and far between, and Sweden's opiate substitution therapy is also opposed in many quarters, though it is available. Compounding the limited availability of some services for people who use drugs, such services often have high thresholds for eligibility and are marked by conditionality of services, with reports of services being punitively withheld and people who use drugs being excluded, punished, and/or disciplined if they do not comply with rules and regulations, and/or if they fail to conform to expectations of normatively acceptable behaviour. Swedish services thus operate as projects which are designed to normalise people who use drugs, constructed, pathologised, and infantalised as unreliable, irrational, dishonest, and sick.

Sweden's drug law and policy informing discourse and service provision has had considerable and detrimental impacts upon the welfare, wellbeing, and health of people who use drugs in Sweden. A lack of service provision, harm reduction, and harm reduction education has resulted in very high rates of drug-related overdoses and overdose fatalities. People share and reuse their needles due to a lack of appropriate service provision, leading to extremely high prevalence and incidence of hepatitis C amongst communities of people who inject drugs, and resulting in other impacts on health and wellbeing. Additionally, people who use drugs have been denied hepatitis C treatment whilst their drug use continues, denying potentially life-saving treatment to those very communities who bear the burden of infection due to Sweden's failure to provide appropriate services and harm reduction.

Compounding these barriers to health and healthcare are the direct impacts of Sweden's criminalising legislation: though it was emphasised when the legislation was introduced in 1988 that it would serve only as a means with which to assist and protect people who use drugs, reports of police-perpetrated violence are all-too common, and people who use drugs routinely experience problematic and stigmatising encounters with Swedish police, coupled with difficulties in reporting crime and abuse, all despite official assurances of the 'good intentions' of the Swedish police and security services in protecting the rights and wellbeing of people who use drugs. And it is perhaps unsurprising that Sweden's repressive criminalisation of people who use drugs, coupled with endemic stigma, discrimination, and social exclusion serves as a disincentive for people who use drugs (and their communities and families) to seek assistance from service and healthcare providers, or the Swedish authorities and police.

In summary of my findings, then, people who use drugs in Sweden are constructed as being deviant, sick, criminal, and unreliable, and drugs (other than snus and alcohol) are generalised as irreconcilably and immutably dangerous. Yet it is the plethora of laws and policies that make the lives of people who use drugs so difficult, that exacerbate harms associated with drug use instead of reducing and ameliorating them, that criminalise and heavily stigmatise people who use drugs to such an extent that managing a stable and healthy life becomes all but impossible. In short, the Swedish model on drugs is something of a circularly self-perpetuating vicious circle: Sweden makes drug use dangerous, and uses this to justify legislation and policy that makes drug use dangerous; Sweden makes drug users' lives extremely dangerous and difficult, and uses this to justify radically invasive, controlling, and criminalising approaches.

Sweden's 'drug-free society': a utopian solution for all the world?

Despite all of this, Sweden continues to advocate in favour of its drug legislation, falsely positioning itself as having successfully addressed the constructed problem of drug use. This is not only the case in terms of Sweden's drug policy, but other laws and policies also, which Sweden seems to use to position itself and posture on an international stage as a state that takes a strong, clear-cut, and radical stand on frequently divisive issues. But that, perhaps, is the very issue: these issues are divisive because they are complex, intricate, and nuanced.

There are no clear cut answers, and as the second respondent that I quote below emphasises, the situation in Sweden – a state that has about the same population as London – is, of course, very different from the situation elsewhere. Even *had* Swedish drug policy succeeded in its outspoken ambition of reducing drug use in Sweden considerably (for which there is no good evidence) and done so without considerably exacerbating difficulties, dangers, and harms for people who use drugs (which I hope to have demonstrated has not been the case), the Swedish model on drug policy (or other phenomena and activities for that matter) cannot simply be advocated as a magic bullet to be deployed in other contexts, cultures, and situations in which various drugs and patterns and histories of drug use diverge starkly from Sweden's experience. And so why does Sweden – a relatively small state in terms of population – come to position itself thus, as – per the second quotation below – 'special'? It is arguably Sweden's past that informs how it instructs other states to construct their futures. Sweden's history of violent social engineering and projects of *modernity* and *rationalisation* have come to inform Sweden's view of itself as a bastion of rational progression for the world to follow, with this going hand-in-hand with Sweden's fear of foreign influence.

> 'It's so difficult to say, "It's like this in Sweden" or "It's like this in France, or in Italy, or even the UK"... I realised why this view on Sweden is so established on the international and European level. It's because that the Swedes, the politicians who work on United Nation level, and European Union level, sell the Swedish model as the world's best... and other countries, they don't speak out that loud that they have the world's best drug policy, so the eyes are focussed on Sweden and on our laws.'
>
> (Interview, Chair and Founder of *Svenska Brukarföreningen*; also quoted in Levy 2015)

> 'Because [in Sweden it's thought that] we are special. We know how to do things. And we don't really care about what they do in the rest of the world… we should go outside our own country and tell everybody how to deal with these kind of issues. And what we told was that we were in control. We were in control. But we didn't have the same situation as, for instance, in the UK or other European countries… But that is a picture that our politicians love to show, that we have dealt with it in a way that is better than anyone else.'
>
> (Interview, Chair of RFHL; also quoted in Levy 2015)

In summary: Sweden's war on people who use drugs

It is not particularly original to note that harms associated with drug use are exacerbated, driven, and actually created by prohibition, criminalisation, stigma and discrimination, and by the so-called war on drugs. Pursuit of prohibition has resulted in social exclusion, displacement, violence, discrimination, and exacerbated stigmatisation of people who use drugs the world over.

Sweden, though, as I began this book by emphasising, has a distinctly 'liberal' and 'progressive' reputation, and is therefore often assumed to diverge from conservative approaches. Sweden is often identified as a benchmark of liberal and successful socialist democracy, a state seen to be one that prioritises the wellbeing and social inclusion of its citizens, a state that would surely promote these same policies of inclusion and empowerment for people in Sweden who use drugs, a community who experience criminalisation, stigmatisation, and discrimination globally and routinely.

Yet Sweden's criminalising and punitive drug legislation is in absolute contrast to Sweden's reputation as a progressive 'liberal' society. Despite paying lip-service to offering compassion and protection for people who use drugs, Sweden's war on drugs and Sweden's aspiration for a drug-free society have, in reality, resulted in a war on the people who use drugs themselves, a war on their health, wellbeing, and social inclusion.

Sweden's progressive, liberal reputation is ill-deserved, arguably entirely misrepresentative. Sweden is a state still shaped by legacies of social control, eugenics, violent social engineering, and aggressive projects of modernity. It is Sweden's history that shapes contemporary law and policy pertaining to people who use drugs and other marginalised communities, with Sweden's legacies conspiring to shape moral panics in Sweden, and with these fears and concerns feeding into popular concerns about drugs and the people who use them.

And Sweden's history has shaped how people who use drugs are treated by the People's Home, the *folkhemmet*, with their being displaced, contained, controlled, and fastidiously socially excluded from the normative (and exclusive) Swedish welfare state. Sweden's fear of destabilising, deviant populations has resulted in the adoption of an extreme model of criminalisation and pathologisation of people who use drugs in an attempt to realise an impossible goal of a drug-free society. Sweden has failed to achieve its misguided ambition, all at the expense of, and without any regard for, the wellbeing of those to whom legislation pertains: people who use drugs.

Bibliography

Abdul-Quader, A. S., Heckathorn, D. D., Sabin, K., and Saidel, T., 2006, Implementation and Analysis of Respondent Driven Sampling: Lessons Learned from the Field. *Journal of Urban Health*83: 1–5

Advisory Council on the Misuse of Drugs, 2009, *The Primary Prevention of Hepatitis C Among Injecting Drug Users* (London: Home Office)

Ahern, J., Stuber, J., and Galea, S., 2007, Stigma, Discrimination and the Health of Illicit Drug Users. *Drug and Alcohol Dependence*88: 188–196

Ahmed, D. A. A., 2011, Issues of Gender, Reflexivity and Positionality in the Field of Disability: Researching Visual Impairment in an Arab Society. *Qualitative Social Work* 10, 4: 467–484

AIVL (Australian Injecting & Illicit Drug Users League), 2006, *A Framework For Peer Education By Drug-User Organisations* (Canberra: AIVL)

Amnesty International, 1997, *Sweden Osmo Vallo – Action Needed to Prevent more Deaths in Custody* (AI Index: EUR 42/01/97), available at http://www.amnesty.org/en/library/info/EUR42/001/1997/en (last accessed 21/10/11)

Amundsen, E. J., 2006, Measuring Effectiveness of Needle and Syringe Exchange Programmes for Prevention of HIV among Injecting Drug Users. *Addiction* 101: 911–912

Amundsen, E. J., Eskild, A., Stigum, H., Smith, E., and Aalen, O. O., 2003, Legal Access to Needles and Syringes/Needle Exchange programmes versus HIV Counselling and Testing to Prevent Transmission of HIV among Intravenous Drug Users: A Comparative Study of Denmark, Norway and Sweden. *European Journal of Public Health* 13: 252–258

Anker, J., 2007, Limits and Opportunities for Autonomous User Organisations in Denmark and Sweden. *Journal of Social Sciences* 3, 2: 78–87

Atkinson, P., and Hammersley, M., 1994, Ethnography and Participant Observation, in *Handbook of Qualitative Research*, ed. Denzin, N. K., and Lincoln, Y. S.: 248–261 (Thousand Oaks, CA: Sage)

Baldwin, P., 1999, *Contagion and the State in Europe: 1830–1930* (Cambridge: Cambridge University Press)

Baldwin, P., 2005, *Disease and Democracy: The Industrialized World Faces AIDS* (London: University of California Press)

Başoğlu, M., Mineka, S., Paker, M., Aker, T., Livanou, M., and Gök, Ş., 1997, Psychological Preparedness for Trauma as a Protective Factor in Survivors of Torture. *Psychological Medicine* 27: 1421–1433

Becker, H. S., 1958, Problems of Inference and Proof in Participant Observation. *American Sociological Review* 23, 6: 652–660

Becker, H. S., and Geer, B., 1957, Participant Observation and Interviewing: A Comparison. *Human Organisation* 16, 3: 28–32

Bejerot, N., 1972, A Theory of Addiction as an Artificially Induced Drive. *The American Journal of Psychiatry* 128, 7: 842–846

Bersani, L., 1988, Is the Rectum a Grave? in *AIDS: Cultural Analysis, Cultural Activism*, ed. Crimp, D. (Cambridge MA: MIT Press)

Blom, I., 2006, Fighting Venereal Diseases: Scandinavian Legislation c.1800 to c.1950. *Medical History* 50: 209–234

Blom, I., 2007, Contagion and Cultural Perceptions of Accepted Behaviour: Tuberculosis and Venereal Diseases in Scandinavia c.1900–c.1950. *Hygiea Internationalis* 6, 2: 121–133

Bluthenthal, R. N., Kral, A. H., Gee, L., Erringer, E. A., and Edlin, B. R., 2000, The Effect of Syringe Exchange Use on High-risk Injection Drug Users: A Cohort Study. *AIDS* 14: 605–611

Boekhout van Solinge, T., 1997, *The Swedish Drug Control System: An In-depth Review and Analysis* (Amsterdam: Jan Mets Centre for Drug Research, University of Amsterdam)

Brooks-Gordon, B., 2006, *The Price of Sex* (Cullompton: Willan Publishing)

Bruggmann, P., Broers, B., and Meili, D., 2007, Hepatitis C Treatment in Patients Receiving Opiate Substitution: Recommendations of the Swiss Association for Addiction Medicine. *Swiss Medical Forum* 7: 916–919

Buchanan, J., and Young, L., 2000, The War on Drugs – A War on Drug Users? *Drugs: Education, Prevention Policy* 7, 4: 409–422

Burgess, R. G., 1981, Keeping a Research Diary. *Cambridge Journal of Education* 11, 1: 75–83

Butler, J., 2004, *Undoing Gender* (Abingdon: Routledge)

Byrne, J., and Albers, E. R., 2010, Coexisting or Conjoined: The Growth of the International Drug Users' Movement through Participation with International Harm Reduction Association Conferences. *International Journal of Drug Policy* 21: 110–111

Caldicott, D. G. E., Edwards, N. A., Kruys, A., Kirkbride, K. P., Sims, N., Byard, R. W., Prior, M., and Irvine, R. J., 2003, Dancing with 'Death': P-Methoxyamphetamine Overdose and Its Acute Management. *Journal of Toxicology Clinical Toxicology* 41, 2: 143–154

Clausen, V., 2007, *An Assessment of Gunilla Ekberg's Account of Swedish Prostitution Policy*, available at http://www.sexworkeurope.org/sites/default/files/resource-pdfs/ekberg_kritik.pdf (last accessed 16/11/13)

Cohen, P., 2006, Looking at the UN, Smelling a Rat. *Amsterdam Law Forum* 2, 4: 75–84

Cohen, S., 1972, *Folk Devils and Moral Panics – The Creation of the Mods and the Rockers* (London: MacGibbon & Kee)

Cusick, L., Kinnell, H., Brooks-Gordon, B., and Campbell, R., 2009, Wild Guesses and Conflated Meanings? Estimating the Size of the Sex Worker Population in Britain. *Critical Social Policy* 29, 4: 703–719

Cwikel, J., and Hoban, E., 2005, Contentious Issues in Research on Trafficked Women Working in the Sex Industry: Study Design, Ethics, and Methodology. *The Journal of Sex Research* 42: 306–316

Danna, D., 2012, Client-Only Criminalization in the City of Stockholm: A Local Research on the Application of the 'Swedish Model' of Prostitution Policy. *Sexuality Research and Social Policy* 9, 1: 80–93

Danziger, R., 1999, The Social Impact of HIV Testing: A Comparative Analysis of Britain and Sweden. *Social Science & Medicine* 48: 293–300

Darke, S., and Hall, W., 2003, Heroin-Overdose: Research and Evidence-Based Intervention. *Journal of Urban Health: Bulletin of the New York Academy of Medicine* 80, 2: 189–200

Davoli, M., Bargagli, A. M., Perucci, C. A., Schifano, P., Belleudi, V., Hickman, M., Salamina, G., Diecidue, R., Vigna-Taglianti, F., and Faggiano, F., 2007, Risk of Fatal Overdose during and after Specialist Drug Treatment: The VEdeTTE Study, a National Multi-site Prospective Cohort Study. *Addiction* 102: 1954–1959

Day, C., and Topp, L., 2003, Safety in Drug and Alcohol Research. *Addiction* 98, 12: 1641–1643

Dean, M., 1994, *Critical and Effective Histories: Foucault's Methods and Historical Sociology* (London: Routledge)

Dean, M., 2002, Liberal Government and Authoritarianism. *Economy and Society* 31, 1: 37–61

Deering, K. N., Amin, A., Shoveller, J., Nesbitt, A., Garcia-Moreno, C., Duff, P., Argento, E., and Shannon, K., 2014, A Systematic Review of the Correlates of Violence Against Sex Workers. *American Journal of Public Health* 104, 5: e42–54

Degenhardt, L., and Hall, W., 2012, Extent of Illicit Drug Use and Dependence, and Their Contribution to the Global Burden of Disease. *The Lancet* 379: 55–70

Des Jarlais, D. C., 1995, Editorial: Harm Reduction: A Framework for Incorporating Science into Drug Policy. *American Journal of Public Health* 85: 10–12

Des Jarlais, D. C., Paone, D., Friedman, S. R., Peyser, N., and Newman, R. G., 1995, Regulating Controversial Programs for Unpopular People: Methadone Maintenance and Syringe Exchange Programs. *American Journal of Public Health* 85, 11: 1577–1584

Des Jarlais, D. C., Paone, D., Milliken, J., Turner, C. F., Miller, H., Gribble, J., Shi, Q., Hagan, H., and Friedman, S. R., 1999, Audio-computer Interviewing to Measure Risk Behaviour for HIV among Injecting Drug Users: A Quasi-randomised Trial. *The Lancet* 353: 1657–1662

Dodillet, S., 2004, Cultural Clash on Prostitution: Debates on Prostitution in Germany and Sweden in the 1990s. Paper presented at the First Global Conference: Critical Issues in Sexuality, Salzburg, Austria, October

Dolan, K., Wodak, A., and Penny, R., 1995, AIDS behind Bars: Preventing HIV Spread among Incarcerated Drug Injectors. *AIDS* 9: 825–832

Drucker, E., Lurie, P., Wodakt, A., and Alcabes, P., 1998, Measuring Harm Reduction: The Effects of Needle and Syringe Exchange Programs and Methadone Maintenance on the Ecology of HIV. *AIDS* 12: 5217–5230

Eastwood, N., Shiner, M., and Bear, D., 2013, *The Numbers in Black and White: Ethnic Disparities in the Policing and Prosecution of Drug Offences in England and Wales* (Release: London)

Ekerwald, H., 2001, The Modernist Manifesto of Alva and Gunnar Myrdal: Modernization of Sweden in the Thirties and the Question of Sterilization. *International Journal of Politics, Culture, and Society* 14, 3: 539–561

Ellsberg, M., and Heise, L., 2002, Bearing Witness: Ethics in Domestic Violence Research. *The Lancet* 359: 1599–1604

Elman, R. A., 2001, Unprotected by the Swedish Welfare State Revisited: Assessing a Decade of Reforms for Battered Women. *Women's Studies International Forum* 24: 39–52

Elwood, S. A. and Martin, D. G., 2000, 'Placing' Interviews: Location and Scales of Power in Qualitative Research. *Professional Geographer* 52, 4: 649–659

EMCDDA (European Monitoring Centre for Drugs and Drug Addiction), 2008, *Sweden: New Development, Trends and In-depth Information on Selected Issues* (Luxembourg: Office of Official Publications of the European Communities)

EMCDDA (European Monitoring Centre for Drugs and Drug Addiction), 2009, *Annual Report 2009: The State of the Drugs Problem in Europe* (Luxembourg: Publications Office of the European Union)

EMCDDA (European Monitoring Centre for Drugs and Drug Addiction), 2010, *Country Overview: Sweden*, available at http://www.emcdda.europa.eu/publications/country-overviews/se#harm (last accessed 25/10/11)

EMCDDA (European Monitoring Centre for Drugs and Drug Addiction), 2011, *Statistical Bulletin 2011 Table DRD-2*, available at http://www.emcdda.europa.eu/stats11/drdtab2a (last accessed 12/01/12)

Faden, R., Geller, G., and Powers, M., 1991, *AIDS, Women, and the Next Generation: Towards a Morally Acceptable Public Policy for HIV Testing of Pregnant Women and Newborns* (New York: Oxford University Press)

Farley, M., 2004, 'Bad for the Body, Bad for the Heart': Prostitution Harms Women Even if Legalized or Decriminalized. *Violence Against Women* 10: 1087–1125

Farley, M., 2006, Prostitution, Trafficking, and Cultural Amnesia: What We Must Not Know in Order to Keep the Business of Sexual Exploitation Running Smoothly. *Yale Journal of Law and Feminism* 18: 101–136

Folkhälsomyndigheten, 2015, *Hälsofrämjande och förebyggande arbete med hepatit och hiv för personer som injicerar droger – En Vägledning*, available at https://www.folkhalsomyndigheten.se/pagefiles/19347/H%C3%A4lsofr%C3%A4mjande-f%C3%B6rebyggande-hepatit-hiv-personer-injicerar-droger-15001.pdf (last accessed 29/12/16)

Foucault, M., 1979/1975, *Discipline and Punish: The Birth of the Prison* (London: Penguin)

Foucault, M., 1976, *The History of Sexuality: The Will to Knowledge* (London: Penguin)

Foucault, M., 1981, The Order of Discourse – Inaugural Lecture at the Collège de France, given 2 December 1970, in *Untying the Text: A Poststructuralist Reader*, ed. Young, R. (London: Routledge)

Fox, D. M., Day, P., and KleinR., 1989, The Power of Professionalism: Policies for AIDS in Britain, Sweden, and the United States. *Daedalus* 118, 2: 93–112

Furberg, H., Bulik, C. M., Lerman, C., Lichtenstein, P., Pedersen, N. L., and Sullivan, P. F., 2005, Is Swedish Snus Associated with Smoking Initiation or Smoking Cessation? *Tobacco Control* 14: 422–424

Gartner, C. E., Hall, W. D., Vos, T., Bertram, M. Y., Wallace, A. L., and Lim, S. S., 2007, Assessment of Swedish Snus for Tobacco Harm Reduction: An Epidemiological Modelling Study. *The Lancet* 369: 2010–2014

Gibson, D. R., Flynn, N. M., and McCarthy, J. J., 1999, Effectiveness of Methadone Treatment in Reducing HIV Risk Behavior and HIV Seroconversion among Injecting Drug Users. *AIDS* 13: 1807–1818

Glaser, B. G., and Strauss, A. L., 1967, *The Discovery of Grounded Theory: Strategies for Qualitative Research* (London: Transaction Publishers)

Global Commission on Drug Policy, 2011, *War on Drugs: Report of the Global Commission on Drug Policy*, available at http://www.globalcommissionondrugs.org/wp-content/themes/gcdp_v1/pdf/Global_Commission_Report_English.pdf (last accessed 17/11/13)

Global Commission on Drug Policy, 2012, *The War on Drugs and HIV/AIDS: How the Criminalization of Drug Use Fuels the Global Pandemic*, available at http://www.globalcommissionondrugs.org/reports/the-war-on-drugs-and-hivaids/ (last accessed 28/06/12)

Global Commission on Drug Policy, 2013, *The Negative Impact of the War on Drugs on Public Health: The Hidden Hepatitis C Epidemic*, available at http://www.globalcommissionondrugs.org/hepatitis/gcdp_hepatitis_english.pdf (last accessed 17/06/13)

Goffman, E., 1968, *Stigma: Notes on the Management of Spoiled Identity* (London: Pelican Books)

Gould, A., 1989, Cleaning the People's Home: Recent Developments in Sweden's Addiction Policy. *British Journal of Addiction* 84: 731–741

Gould, A., 1996, Drug Issues and the Swedish Press. *The International Journal of Drug Policy* 7, 2, available at http://www.drugtext.org/library/articles/96724.htm (last accessed 21/10/11)

Gould, A., 2001, The Criminalisation of Buying Sex: the Politics of Prostitution in Sweden. *Journal of Social Policy* 30, 3: 437–456

Gould, A., 2005, Resisting Postmodernity: Swedish Social Policy in the 1990s. *Social Work & Society* 3, 1: 72–84

Hallam, C., 2010, What We Can Learn from Sweden's Drug Policy Experience. *The Beckley Foundation Drug Policy Programme*: 1–11

Harm Reduction International, n.d. *What is Harm Reduction? A Position Statement from Harm Reduction International*, available at http://www.ihra.net/what-is-harm-reduction (last accessed 17/12/15)

Harrington, C., 2012, Prostitution Policy Models and Feminist Knowledge Politics in New Zealand and Sweden. *Sexuality Research and Social Policy* 9, 4: 337–349. doi:10.1007/s13178-012-0083-4

Health Protection Agency, Health Protection Scotland, National Public Health Service for Wales, Communicable Disease Surveillance Centre Northern Ireland, Centre for Research on Drugs & Health Behaviour, 2008, *Shooting Up: Infections among Injecting Drug Users in the United Kingdom 2007 – An Update* (London: Health Protection Agency)

Heckathorn, D. D., 1997, Respondent-Driven Sampling: A New Approach to the Study of Hidden Populations. *Social Problems* 44, 2: 174–199

Heckathorn, D. D., Semaan, S., Broadhead, R. S., and Hughes, J. J., 2002, Extensions of Respondent-Driven Sampling: A New Approach to the Study of Injection Drug Users Aged18–25. *AIDS and Behavior* 6, 1: 55–67

Hedrich, D., Kerr, T., and Dubois-Arber, F., 2010, Drug Consumption Facilities in Europe and Beyond, in *European Monitoring Centre for Drugs and Drug Addiction, Harm Reduction: Evidence, Impacts and Challenges*, ed. Rhodes, T., and Hedrich, D.: 305–331 (Luxembourg: Publications Office of the European Union)

Henriksson, B., and Ytterberg, H., 1992, Sweden: The Power of the Moral(istic) Left, in *AIDS in the Industrialized Democracies: Passions, Politics and Policies*, ed. Kirp, D. L., and Bayer, R.: 317–338 (New Brunswick: Rutgers University Press)

Homan, R., 1980, The Ethics of Covert Methods. *The British Journal of Sociology*, 31, 1, 46–59

Home Affairs Minutes of Evidence (House of Commons), 2002, *MR Ralf Löfstedt, Deputy Director of the Ministry of Health and Social Affairs, Sweden, Examined*, available at http://www.publications.parliament.uk/pa/cm200102/cmselect/cmhaff/318/2031901.htm (last accessed 12/04/12)

Home Office, 2012, *Putting Full Recovery First: the Recovery Roadmap*, available at http://www.homeoffice.gov.uk/publications/alcohol-drugs/drugs/recovery-roadmap (last accessed 11/05/12)

Howell, P., 2007, Foucault, Sexuality, Geography, in *Space, Knowledge and Power: Foucault and Geography*, ed. Crampton, J. W., and Elden, S.: 291–315 (Aldershot: Ashgate)

Hubbard, P., 1999, Researching Female Sex Work: Reflections on Geographical Exclusion, Critical Methodologies and 'Useful' Knowledge. *Area* 31, 3: 229–237

Hubbard, P., Matthews, R., and Scoular, J., 2007a, *Regulating the Spaces of Sex Work in the EU: Regulation of Sex Work in Sweden* (Loughborough: University of Loughborough)

Hubbard, P., Matthews, R., and Scoular, J., 2007b, *Regulating the Spaces of Sex Work: Assessing the Impact of Prostitution Law. Full Research Report* (Swindon: ESRC)

Hunt, N., Albert, E., and Montañés Sánchez, V., 2010, User Involvement and User Organising in Harm Reduction, in *Harm Reduction: Evidence, Impacts and Challenges*, EMCDDA Scientific Monograph Series No. 10, ed. Rhodes, T., and Hedrich, D.: 369–392 (Luxembourg: Publications Office of the European Union)

Hurley, S. F., Jolley, D. J., and Kaldor, J. M., 1997, Effectiveness of Needle-exchange Programmes for Prevention of HIV Infection. *The Lancet* 349: 1797–1800

INPUD, 2011, *INPUD Position Statement on Language, Identity, Inclusivity and Discrimination*, available at https://inpud.wordpress.com/position-papers/inpud-position-statement-on-language-identity-inclusivity-and-discrimination/ (last accessed 20/02/17)

INPUD, 2014a, *Drug User Peace Initiative: Violations of the Human Rights of People who Use Drugs*, available at https://www.unodc.org/documents/ungass2016/Contributions/Civil/INPUD/DUPI-Violations_of_the_Human_Rights_of_People_Who_Use_Drugs-Web.pdf (last accessed 06/10/16)

INPUD, 2014b, *Drug User Peace Initiative – A War on the Health of People who UseDrugs*, available at http://www.druguserpeaceinitiative.org/dupidocuments/DUPI-A_War_on_the_Health_of_People_who_Use_Drugs.pdf (last accessed 11/12/15)

INPUD, 2015, *Consensus Statement on Drug Use under Prohibition: Human Rights, Health, and the Law* (London: INPUD) available at https://www.inpud.net/consensus_statement_2015.pdf (last accessed 10/01/15)

International Federation of Red Cross and Red Crescent Societies, 2003, *Spreading the Light of Science: Guidelines on Harm Reduction Related to Injecting Drug Use* (Geneva: International Federation of Red Cross and Red Crescent Societies)

International Sex Worker Harm Reduction Caucus, 2008, Statement. International Harm Reduction Association's 19th International Conference Harm Reduction 2008, Barcelona, Spain, 11–15 May

Jeffreys, S., 1997, *The Idea of Prostitution* (Melbourne: Spinifex Press)

Jellinek, E. M., 1960, *The Disease Concept of Alcoholism* (New Haven: Hillhouse Press)

Jick, T. J., 1979, Mixing Qualitative and Quantitative Methods: Triangulation in Action. *Administrative Science Quarterly* 24, 4: 602–611

Jorgensen, J. L., 1989, *Participant Observation: A Methodology for Human Studies* (California: SAGE Publications)

Jürgens, R., 2008, *'Nothing about us without us' – Greater, Meaningful Involvement of People who Use Illegal Drugs: A Public Health, Ethical, and Human Rights Imperative*, International edition, available at http://www.aidsalliance.org/assets/000/000/376/310-1.-Nothing-about-us-without-us-Report-(English)_original.pdf?1405520211 (last accessed 20/02/17)

Jürgens, R., Csete, J., Amon, J. J., Baral, S., and Beyrer, C., 2010, People Who Use Drugs, HIV, and Human Rights. *The Lancet*376: 475–485. doi:10.1016/S0140–6736(10)60830–6

Käll, K., Hermansson, U., Amundsen, E. J., Rönnbäck, K., and Rönnberg, S., 2007, The Effectiveness of Needle Exchange Programmes for HIV Prevention: A Critical Review. *The Journal of Global Drug Policy and Practice* 1, 3, available at http://www.globaldrugpolicy.org/Issues/Vol%201%20Issue%203/The%20Effectiveness%20of%20Needle%20Exchange.pdf (last accessed 21/11/16)

Kayal, P. M., 1993, *Bearing Witness: Gay Men's Health Crisis and the Politics of AIDS* (Boulder CO: Westview Press)

Keane, H., 2002, *What's Wrong with Addiction?* (Melbourne: Melbourne University Press)

Keane, H., 2009, Foucault on Methadone: Beyond Biopower. *International Journal of Drug Policy* 20: 450–452

Kerr, T., and Wood, E., 2008, Misrepresentation of Science Undermines HIV Prevention. *Canadian Medical Association Journal* 178, 7: 964

Kilvington, J., Day, S., and Ward, H., 2001, Prostitution Policy in Europe: A Time of Change? *Feminist Review* 67: 78–93

Kirp, D. L., and Bayer, R., 1992, Introduction: An Epidemic in Political and Policy Perspective, in *AIDS in the Industrialized Democracies: Passions, Politics and Policies*, ed. Kirp, D. L., and Bayer, R.: 1–6 (New Brunswick: Rutgers University Press)

Kulick, D., 2003, Sex in the New Europe: The Criminalization of Clients and Swedish Fear of Penetration. *Anthropological Theory* 3: 199–218

Kulick, D., 2005, Four Hundred Thousand Swedish Perverts. *GLQ* 11, 2: 205–235

Kurtz, S. P., Surratt, H. L., Kiley, M. C., and Inciardi, J. A., 2005, Barriers to Health and Social Services for Street-Based Sex Workers. *Journal of Health Care for the Poor and Underserved* 16: 345–361

Larkin, M., Wood, R. T. A., and Griffiths, M. D., 2006, Towards Addiction as Relationship. *Addiction Research and Theory* 14, 3: 207–215

Lenke, L., and Olsson, B., 2002, Swedish Drug Policy in the Twenty-First Century: A Policy Model Going Astray. *Annals of the American Academy of Political and Social Science* 582: 64–79

Lennie, J., Hatcher, C., and Morgan, W., 2003, Feminist Discourses of (Dis)empowerment in an Action Research Project Involving Rural Women and Communication Technologies. *Action Research* 1, 1: 57–80

Levy, J., 2011, Impacts of the Swedish Criminalisation of the Purchase of Sex on Service Provision for Sex Workers. Correlation Conference, Ljubljana, 12–14 December, 2011, available at http://correlation-net.org/correlation_conference/images/Presentations/MS4_Levy.pdf (last accessed 03/06/13)

Levy, J., 2013, *The Harms of Drug Use: Criminalisation, Misinformation, and Stigma* (INPUD and Youth Rise)

Levy, J., 2015, *Criminalising the Purchase of Sex: Lessons from Sweden* (Abingdon: Routledge)

Levy, J., and Jakobsson, P., 2013, Abolitionist Feminism as Patriarchal Control: Swedish Understandings of Prostitution and Trafficking. *Dialectical Anthropology* 37, 2: 333–340

Levy, J., Smith, D., St.John-Green, C., 2013, *PMA Contaminated Ecstasy and MDMA Alert for MDMA and Ecstasy Users* (London: INPUD) available at http://www.inpud.net/PMA_Warning_INPUD_Oct2013.pdf (last accessed 07/01/16)

Lidman, C., Norden, L., Kåberg, M., Käll, K., Franck, J., Aleman, S., and Birk, M., 2009, Hepatitis C Infection among Injection Drug Users in Stockholm Sweden: Prevalence and Gender. *Scandinavian Journal of Infectious Diseases* 41: 679–684

Lindberg, O., and Haynes, P., 2000, *A Comparison of Drug Treatment Policy in Britain and Sweden: Politics, Culture and Elite Interest Groups* (Qualitative European Drug Research Network), available at http://qed.emcdda.eu.int/journal/papers2.shtml (last accessed 22/01/10)

Linton, M., 2011, *Nu Rasar Grunden för Svensk Drogpolitik*, available at http://www.dn.se/kultur-noje/debatt-essa/nu-rasar-grunden-for-svensk-drogpolitik (last accessed 20/10/11)

Ljungberg, B., Christensson, B., Tunving, K., Bengt, A., Landvall, B., Lundberg, M., and Zäll-Friberg, A., 1991, HIV Prevention Among Injecting Drug Users: Three Years of Experience from a Syringe Exchange Program in Sweden. *Journal of Acquired Immune Deficiency Syndromes* 4: 890–895

Logie, C. H., James, L., Tharao, W., and Loutfy, M. R., 2011, HIV, Gender, Race, Sexual Orientation, and Sex Work: A Qualitative Study of Intersectional Stigma Experienced by HIV-Positive Women in Ontario, Canada. *PLoS Med* 8, 11: e1001124. doi:10.1371/journal.pmed.1001124

Lundberg, A., 2006, Legislation on Venereal Disease. Lex Veneris1919–1945 . *Sven Med Tidskr* 10, 1: 125–144

Månsson, A. S., Moestrup, T., Nordenfelt, E., and Widell, A., 2000, Continued Transmission of Hepatitis B and C Viruses, But No Transmission of Human Immunodeficiency Virus Among Intravenous Drug Users Participating in a Syringe/Needle Exchange Program. *Scandinavian Journal of Infectious Diseases* 32: 253–258

Mathers, B. M., Degenhardt, L., Ali, H., Wiessing, L., Hickman, M., Mattick, R. P., Myers, B., Ambekar, A., and Strathdee, S. A., 2010, HIV Prevention, Treatment, and Care Services for People who Inject Drugs: A Systematic Review of Global, Regional, and National Coverage. *The Lancet* 375, 9719: 1014–1028. doi:10.1016/S0140-6736(10)60232-2

McCarney, J., 2005, Ideology and False Consciousness. *Marx Myths and Legends*, available at http://www.marxmyths.org/joseph-mccarney/article.htm (last accessed 11/09/12)

Nelson, P. K., Mathers, B. M., Cowie, B., Hagan, H., Des Jarlais, D., Horyniak, D., and Degenhardt, L., 2011, Global Epidemiology of Hepatitis B and Hepatitis C in People who Inject Drugs: Results of Systematic Reviews. *The Lancet* 378, 9791: 571–583

Ning, A. M., 2005, Games of Truth: Rethinking Conformity and Resistance in Narratives of Heroin Recovery. *Medical Anthropology* 24, 4: 349–382

Norden, L., Van Veen, M., Lidman, C., Todorov, I., Guarita, B., Kretzschmar, M., and Wiessing, L., 2013, Hepatitis C Among Injecting Drug Users Is Two Times Higher in Stockholm, Sweden than in Rotterdam, the Netherlands. *Substance Use & Misuse* 48, 14: 1469–1474.

Noy, C., 2008, Sampling Knowledge: The Hermeneutics of Snowball Sampling in Qualitative Research. *International Journal of Social Research Methodology* 11, 4: 327–344

Nutt, D., 2009, David Nutt: My Views on Drugs Classification. *The Guardian*, 3 November, available at http://www.guardian.co.uk/uk/2009/nov/03/david-nutt-drugs-policy (last accessed 17/06/13)

Nutt, D., King, L. A., and Phillips, L. D., on behalf of the Independent Scientific Committee on Drugs, 2010, Drug Harms in the UK: A Multicriteria Decision Analysis. *The Lancet* 376, 9752: 1558–1565

Nutt, D., King, L. A., Saulsbury, W., and Blakemore, C., 2007, Development of a Rational Scale to Assess the Harm of Drugs of Potential Misuse. *The Lancet* 369: 1047–1053

Open Society Institute, 2009, *At What Cost? HIV and Human Rights Consequences of the Global 'War on Drugs'* (New York: Open Society Institute), available at https://www.opensocietyfoundations.org/sites/default/files/at-what-cost_20090302.pdf (last accessed 20/02/17)

Östergren, P., 2004, Sexworkers' Critique of Swedish Prostitution Policy, available at http://www.petraostergren.com/pages.aspx?r_id=40716 (last accessed 31/03/12)

Östergren, P., and Dodillet, S., 2011, The Swedish Sex Purchase Act: Claimed Success and Documented Effects. Presented at The International Workshop: Decriminalizing Prostitution and Beyond: Practical Experiences and Challenges. The Hague, 3–4 March

Patrick, D. M., Tyndall, M. W., Cornelisse, P. G. A., Li, K., Sherlock, C. H., Rekart, M. L., Strathdee, S. A., Currie, S. L., Schechter, M. T., O'Shaughnessy, M. V., 2001, Incidence of Hepatitis C Virus Infection among Injection Drug Users during an Outbreak of HIV Infection. *CMAJ* 165, 7: 889–895

Pennycook, A., 1994, Incommensurable Discourses? *Applied Linguistics* 15, 2: 115–138

Pidd, H., 2013, Further Arrests over 'Contaminated' Ecstasy Deaths. *The Guardian*, 23 January, available at http://www.usq.edu.au/library/referencing/harvard-agps-referencing-guide#Jnl&News (last accessed 12/03/13)

Pred, A., 2000, *Even in Sweden: Racisms, Racialized Spaces, and the Popular Imagination* (London: University of California Press)

Press Association, 2012, Heroin User Infected with Anthrax in Oxford. *The Guardian*, 2 November, available at http://www.guardian.co.uk/world/2012/nov/02/anthrax-infection-heroin-oxford (last accessed 12/03/13)

Pyett, P. M., 2003, Validation of Qualitative Research in the 'Real World'. *Qualitative Health Research* 13, 8: 1170–1179

Raymond, J. G., 2004, Prostitution on Demand: Legalizing the Buyers as Sexual Consumers. *Violence Against Women* 10, 10: 1156–1186

Rehm, J., Sulkowska, U., Mańczuk, M., Boffetta, P., Powles, J., Popova, S., and Zatoński, W., 2007, Alcohol Accounts for a High Proportion of Premature Mortality in Central and Eastern Europe. *International Journal of Epidemiology* 36: 458–467

Reinarman, C., 2005, Addiction as Accomplishment: The Discursive Construction of Disease. *Addiction Research and Theory* 13, 4: 307–320

Rekart, M. L., 2005, Sex-Work Harm Reduction. *The Lancet* 366: 2123–2134

Reuter, P., and Trautmann, F., 2007, *A Report on Global Illicit Drug Markets 1998–2007* European Commission, available at http://ec.europa.eu/justice/anti-drugs/files/report-drug-markets-short_en.pdf (last accessed 08/05/13)

Rhodes, T., Davis, M., and Judd, A., 2004, Hepatitis C and its Risk Management among Drug Injectors in London: Renewing Harm Reduction in the Context of Uncertainty. *Addiction* 99: 621–633

Rhodes, T., Kimber, J., Small, W., Fitzgerald, J., Kerr, T., Hickman, M., and Holloway, G., 2006, Public Injecting and the Need for 'Safer Environment Interventions' in the Reduction of Drug-related Harm. *Addiction* 101: 1384–1393

Rhodes, T., Lowndes, C., Judd, A., Mikhailova, L. A., Sarang, A., Rylkov, A., Tichonov, M., Lewis, K., Ulyanova, N., Alpatova, T., Karavashkin, V., Khutorskoy, M., Hickman, M., Parry, J. V., and Renton, A., 2002, Explosive Spread and High Prevalence of HIV Infection among Injecting Drug Users in Togliatti City, Russia. *AIDS* 16: F25–F31

Room, R., 2005, Stigma, Social Inequality and Alcohol and Drug Use. *Drug and Alcohol Review* 24: 143–155

Sachs, G. A., Hougham, G. W., Sugarman, J., Agre, P., Broome, M. E., Geller, G., Kass, N., Kodish, E., Mintz, J., Roberts, L. W., Sankar, P., Siminoff, L. A., Sorenson, J., and Weiss, A., 2003, Conducting Empirical Research on Informed Consent: Challenges and Questions. *Ethics & Human Research Special Supplement* 25, 5: 1–7

Sandelowski, M., 1994, The Use of Quotes in Qualitative Research. *Research in Nursing & Health* 17, 6: 479–482

Sanders, T., and Campbell, R., 2007, Designing Out Vulnerability, Building in Respect: Violence, Safety and Sex Work Policy. *The British Journal of Sociology* 58: 1–19

Scambler, G., Peswani, R., Adrian, R., and Scambler, A., 1990, Women Prostitutes in the AIDS Era. *Sociology of Health & Illness* 12, 3: 260–273

Seddon, T., 2010, *A History of Drugs: Drugs and Freedom in the Liberal Age* (Abingdon: Routledge)

Shaver, F. M., 2005, Sex Work Research: Methodological and Ethical Challenges. *Journal of Interpersonal Violence* 20, 3: 296–319

Simic, S., Johnston, L. G., Platt, L., Baros, S., Andjelkovic, V., Novotny, T., and Rhodes, T., 2006, *Journal of Urban Health* 83, 7: 6–15

Socialstyrelsen (Swedish National Board of Health and Welfare), 2004, *Prostitution in Sweden 2003: Knowledge, Beliefs & Attitudes Of Key Informants* (www.socialstyrelsen.se)

Socialstyrelsen (Swedish National Board of Health and Welfare), 2008, *Prostitution in Sweden 2007*, available at http://www.socialstyrelsen.se/lists/artikelkatalog/attachments/8806/2008-126-65_200812665.pdf (last accessed 30/09/13)

SOU, 2000, *Steriliseringsfrågan i Sverige 1935–1975 Historisk belysning – Kartläggning – Intervjuer*, available at http://www.regeringen.se/content/1/c4/28/64/212fc81a.pdf (last accessed 07/11/13)

Spice, W., 2007, Management of Sex Workers and other High-risk Groups. *Occupational Medicine* 57: 322–328

Stacey, J., 1988, Can There Be a Feminist Ethnography? *Women's Studies International Forum* 11, 1: 21–27

Stevens, A., 2012, The Ethics and Effectiveness of Coerced Treatment of People who Use Drugs. *Human Rights and Drugs* 2, 1: 7–16

Stevens, A., Stöver, H., and Brentari, C., 2010, Criminal Justice Approaches to Harm Reduction in Europe, in *European Monitoring Centre for Drugs and Drug Addiction, Harm Reduction: Evidence, Impacts and Challenges*, ed. Rhodes, T., and Hedrich, D.: 379–402 (Luxembourg: Publications Office of the European Union)

Stimson, G. V., 1989, Editorial Review – Syringe-Exchange Programmes for Injecting Drug Users. *AIDS* 3: 253–260

Strang, J., McCambridge, J., Best, D., Beswick, T., Bearn, J., Rees, S., and Gossop, M., 2003, Loss of Tolerance and Overdose Mortality after Inpatient Opiate Detoxification: Follow Up Study. *British Medical Journal* 326: 959–960

Subrahmanian, R., 2007, Sexual Politics and Social Policy: Swedish Policy Reviewed in *Reversing the Gaze: Global Perspectives on Nordic Approaches to Gender Equality*, ed. Kabeer, N., Stark, A., and Magnus, E.: 198–243 (London and New York: Routledge)

Svanström, Y., 2006, Prostitution as Vagrancy: Sweden1923–1964. *Journal of Scandinavian Studies in Criminology and Crime Prevention* 7, 2: 142–163

svensktsnus.sehttp://www.svensktsnus.se/en/Snus-Questions–Answers/ (last accessed 30/05/12)

Tammi, T., 2005a, Discipline or Contain? The Struggle over the Concept of Harm Reduction in the 1997 Drug Policy Committee in Finland. *International Journal of Drug Policy* 16: 384–392

Tammi, T., 2005b, Diffusion of Public Health Views on Drug Policy: The Case of Needle Exchange in Finland, in *Beyond Health Literacy: Youth Cultures, Prevention and Policy*, ed. Hoikkala, T., Hakkarainen, P., and Laine, S.: 185–199 (Helsinki: Finnish Youth Research Network, Publications 52 & Stakes)

Tammi, T., and Hurme, T., 2006, How the Harm Reduction Movement Contrasts itself against Punitive Prohibition. *International Journal of Drug Policy* 18, 2: 84–87 doi:10.1016/j.drugpo.2006.11.003

Taylor, M., Mackay, K., Murphy, J., McIntosh, A., McIntosh, C., Anderson, S., and Welch, K., 2012, Quantifying the RR of Harm to Self and Others from Substance

Misuse: Results from a Survey of Clinical Experts across Scotland. *BMJ Open* 2, 4: e000774. doi:10.1136

The Local, 2009, Racist Stereotypes used in Police Training. *The Local*, 7 February, available at http://www.thelocal.se/20090207/17424 (last accessed 29/12/16)

The Local, 2012, Green Light for Needle Exchange in Stockholm. *The Local*, 17 July, available at http://www.thelocal.se/20120717/42064 (last accessed 29/12/16)

UNAIDS, 2009, *UNAIDS Guidance Note on HIV and Sex Work* (Geneva: UNAIDS)

UNODC (United Nations Office on Drugs and Crime), 2008, *Reducing the Adverse Health and Social Consequences of Drug Abuse: A Comprehensive Approach*, available at http://www.unodc.org/documents/prevention/Reducing-adverse-consequences-drug-abuse.pdf (last accessed 26/07/12)

UNODC (United Nations Office on Drugs and Crime), 2011, *World Drug Report 2011*, available at http://www.unodc.org/documents/data-and-analysis/WDR2011/WDR2011-ExSum.pdf (last accessed 18/10/11)

UNODC (United Nations Office on Drugs and Crime), 2006, *Sweden's Successful Drug Policy: A Review of the Evidence*, available at http://www.unodc.org/pdf/research/Swedish_drug_control.pdf (last accessed 17/12/12)

UNODC (United Nations Office on Drugs and Crime), 2014, *World Drug Report* (Vienna: UNODC)

Vallgårda, S., 2007, Problematizations and Path Dependency: HIV/AIDS Policies in Denmark and Sweden . *Medical History* 51: 99–112

Van der Giessen, G. K. T., and Van Brussel, G. H. A., 1996, *Sweden and the Drugs Problem: Seen Through Dutch Eyes*, available at http://www.ukcia.org/research/sweden.htm (last accessed 15/11/10)

Vrecko, S., 2010, 'Civilizing Technologies' and the Control of Deviance. *BioSocieties* 5, 1: 36–51

Wahab, S., 2003, Creating Knowledge Collaboratively with Female Sex Workers: Insights from a Qualitative, Feminist, and Participatory Study. *Qualitative Inquiry* 9: 625–642

Ward, H., 2007, Prostitution: Marxism versus Moralism. *Permanent Revolution*, Winter 2007: 15–21

Watters, J. K., and Biernacki, P., 1989, Targeted Sampling: Options for the Study of Hidden Populations. *Social Problems* 36, 4: 416–430

Weitzer, R., 2008, Legalizing Prostitution: Morality Panics in Western Australia. *British Journal of Criminology* 49: 1–18

WHO (World Health Organization), 2001, *Putting Women First: Ethical and Safety Recommendations for Research on Domestic Violence Against Women* (Geneva: WHO)

WHO (World Health Organization), 2004a, *Highlights on Health in Sweden*, available at http://www.euro.who.int/highlights (last accessed 21/03/12)

WHO (World Health Organization), 2004b, *Effectiveness of Sterile Needle and Syringe Programming in Reducing HIV/AIDS Among Injecting Drug Users* (Geneva: WHO)

WHO (World Health Organization), 2005a, *Effectiveness of Drug Dependence Treatment in Preventing HIV Among Injecting Drug Users* (Geneva: WHO)

WHO (World Health Organization), 2005b, *Violence against Sex Workers and HIV Prevention*, available at http://www.who.int/gender/documents/sexworkers.pdf (last accessed 31/03/12)

WHO (World Health Organization), 2007, *Guide to Starting and Managing Needle and Syringe Programmes* (Geneva: WHO)

WHO (World Health Organization), 2015, *WHO Model List of Essential Medicines* – 19th List (April 2015) (Amended November 2015), available at http://www.who.int/medicines/

publications/essentialmedicines/EML_2015_FINAL_amended_NOV2015.pdf?ua=1 (last accessed 30/12/16)

WHO (World Health Organization), n.d., *Lexicon of Alcohol and Drug Terms Published by the World Health Organization*, available at http://www.who.int/substance_abuse/terminology/who_lexicon/en/ (last accessed 21/04/13)

WHO UNODC UNAIDS (World Health Organization, United Nations Office on Drugs and Crime, and Joint United Nations Programme on HIV/AIDS), 2009, *WHO, UNODC, UNAIDS Technical Guide for Countries to Set Targets for Universal Access to HIV Prevention, Treatment and Care for Injecting Drug Users*, available at http://www.unodc.org/documents/hiv-aids/idu_target_setting_guide.pdf (accessed 10/05/12)

WHO, UNODC, UNAIDS, 2004, *WHO/UNODC/UNAIDS Position Paper: Substitution Maintenance Therapy in the Management of Opioid Dependence and HIV/AIDS Prevention*, available at http://www.who.int/substance_abuse/publications/en/PositionPaper_English.pdf (last accessed 10/11/14)

Wilchins, R., 2004, *Queer Theory, Gender Theory* (Los Angeles: Alyson Books)

Wild, T. C., 2005, Social Control and Coercion in Addiction Treatment: Towards Evidence-based Policy and Practice. *Addiction*101: 40–49

Yap, L., Butler, T., Richters, J., Kirkwood, K., Grant, L., Saxby, M., Ropp, F., and Donovan, B., 2007, Do Condoms Cause Rape and Mayhem? The Long Term Effects of Condoms in New South Wales' Prisons. *Sexually Transmitted Infections* 83, 3: 219–222

Zhu, S. H., Wang, J. B., Hartman, A., Zhuang, Y., Gamst, A., Gibson, J. T., Gilljam, H., and Galanti, M. R., 2009, Quitting Cigarettes Completely or Switching to Smokeless Tobacco: Do US Data Replicate the Swedish Results? *Tobacco Control* 18, 2: 82–87

Zimmerman, C., and Watts, C., 2003, *WHO Ethical and Safety Recommendations for Interviewing Trafficked Women* (Geneva: WHO)

Index

www.ingramcontent.com/pod-product-compliance
Ingram Content Group UK Ltd.
Pitfield, Milton Keynes, MK11 3LW, UK
UKHW011019180926
475701UK00004B/823

* 9 7 8 0 3 6 7 5 9 4 8 5 5 *